# BIFF AT WORK

## YOUR GUIDE TO DIFFICULT WORKPLACE COMMUNICATION

# BIFF

## AT WORK

### YOUR GUIDE TO DIFFICULT WORKPLACE COMMUNICATION

**BILL EDDY,** LCSW, ESQ.
**MEGAN HUNTER,** MBA

**UNHOOKED BOOKS**
*Independent Publishers since 2011*
an imprint of High Conflict Institute Press
Scottsdale, Arizona

**Publisher's Note**
This publication is designed to provide accurate and authoritative information about the subject matters covered. It is sold with the understanding that neither the authors nor publisher are rendering legal, mental health or other professional services, either directly or indirectly. If expert assistance, legal services or counseling is needed, the services of a competent professional should be sought. Neither the authors nor the publisher shall be liable or responsible for any loss or damage allegedly arising as a consequence of your use or application of any information or suggestions in this book.

Cover design by Julian León, The Missive
Interior Design by Jeffrey Fuller, Shelfish

ISBN (print): 978-1950057122
ISBN (ebook): 978-1950057160
Library of Congress Control Number: 2021932787

Unhooked Media, 7701 E. Indian School Rd., Ste. F, Scottsdale, AZ 85251
www.unhookedmedia.com

## Also by Bill Eddy

*It's All Your Fault at Work! Managing Narcissists and other High-Conflict People*

*Hiring Radar*

*Calming Upset People with EAR*

*5 Types of People Who Can Ruin Your Life*

*BIFF: Quick Responses to High Conflict People, Their Personal Attacks and Social Media Meltdowns*

*BIFF for Co-Parent Communication*

*Mediating High Conflict Disputes*

*Why We Elect Narcissists & Sociopaths—and How We Can Stop*

*Dating Radar*

*So, What's Your Proposal*

*It's All Your Fault! 12 Tips for Managing People Who Blame Others for Everything*

*High Conflict People in Legal Disputes*

*Don't Alienate the Kids! Raising Resilient Children While Avoiding High Conflict Divorce*

*Splitting: Protecting Yourself While Divorcing Someone with Borderline or Narcissistic Personality Disorder*

*Managing High Conflict People in Court*

*The Future of Family Court*

*Splitting America*

*New Ways for Families in Separation and Divorce:*
 *Professional Guidebook*
 *Parent Workbook*
 *Collaborative Parent Workbook*
 *Decision Skills Class Instructor's Manual & Workbook*
 *Pre-Mediation Coaching Manual & Workbook*
 *Online Course Coaching Manual*

*New Ways for Work Coaching Manual & Workbook*

*New Ways for Life Instructor Guide & Youth Journal*

## Also by Megan Hunter

*Hiring Radar*

*Dating Radar*

*The Psychology of Notorious Church Killers*

*The High-Conflict Co-Parenting Survival Guide*

*Bait & Switch*

*To all of our clients and colleagues who
do their best to stay reasonable in the
face of hostility and misinformation.*
*—Bill*

*To anyone who has felt the sting upon
reading that one awful email.*
*—Megan*

# Contents

# Introduction

We are excited that you are going to be using BIFF! This is a highly effective and simple method of calming hostile and misinformed conversations in writing, and sometimes in person. Today's workplace is filled with opportunities for anger and misunderstanding to take over, whether from customers, employees, manager, or owners. BIFF gives you a brief way to manage such situations without spending much time and emotional energy at all. In addition, you don't make things worse and you get to feel good about yourself afterward.

BIFF is one of the first techniques that we developed when the two of us starting collaborating in 2007 and co-founded High Conflict Institute in 2008. Bill came into this as a family lawyer with a background as a family therapist, so he knew how badly we needed a method for calming upset families, especially in high conflict divorces. Megan was in policy, legislation and judicial training for the Arizona Supreme Court Administrative Offices of the Courts while earning her MBA.

We met when Megan needed a trainer for family court judges on managing high conflict cases and quite accidentally discovered Bill through a mediation newsletter article. Inviting Bill to train the judges on dealing with people who have high conflict personalities in divorce cases proved successful with the majority of judges remarking about their light bulb moments. Next, Megan invited Bill back to Arizona to provide high conflict training to psychologists involved in family court cases. Expecting around 30-35 attendees, the doors were closed at 200. Again, light bulbs. At that point Megan realized that everyone in the field needed this training and suggested we work together. Thus, the High Conflict Institute was born.

Not surprisingly, our work grew quickly and spread into other segments of society. As it turns out, the people with high conflict divorce cases also create conflict and chaos in their place of work. Our work rapidly grew and continues growing in helping businesses and organizations of all sizes understand and manage high conflict situations and high conflict personalities. With Megan as CEO and Bill as CINO, and a dozen trainers and staff, we are going strong with a worldwide presence. The need for our methods is greater than ever.

Since 2008, we estimate that we have taught at least half a million people the BIFF method, counting BIFF books sold and trainings we have given to workplace professionals and others. We constantly get feedback that those we have trained have taught this method to at least one other person. That means that at least a million people know the BIFF method—so far.

The more people who use it, the easier it is to manage difficult issues without escalating into blamespeak or worse. In fact, it's used so much now that people have turned it from an adjective (a BIFF communication) into a noun (send him a BIFF) and a verb (you better BIFF her before she gets more upset). And it's so easy that you will be BIFF'ing by the time you finish this book. But you will soon discover that it takes practice. BIFF communications are harder than they look at first, but then they get easier and easier as you learn to unhook from the emotion.

In a nutshell, using BIFF in the workplace increases productivity. Instead of spending way too much time perseverating over emails and letters, time can be devoted to the work. Imagine the time saved when everyone in the company uses BIFF consistently in all messaging platforms.

We have written this book in four parts. The first section explains the method. The second section tells how to use it with those external to your work, such as customers and professional clients. The third section gets into workplace issues including those between co-workers, colleagues, employees and managers. Whole organizations have been trained in BIFF and it has benefitted them throughout the workplace as well as in their personal lives. The fourth section explains our BIFF coaching method, so that you can get assistance with your draft BIFF communications, as well as coaching your colleagues with their own BIFFs.

But we believe in being brief, so let's get started.

# SECTION 1

# Understanding
# High Conflict Behaviors

## CHAPTER 1

# Blamespeak

"You're an idiot!" "It's ALL your fault!" "Your work on this is a piece of sh\*\*!" "Don't you have a brain!"

We are living in a culture of blame and disrespect. The language that people use in their work seems to be deteriorating by the day. Since 2008, employee satisfaction surveys have listed other people as the largest source of job stress. "Dealing with my narcissistic boss" has been the number one search term on our website, HighConflictInstitute.com, since 2008, even when our site content was primarily about high-conflict divorce. From co-workers to customers to managers, more and more people feel like they are walking on eggshells around someone in their work. Add to that the rise of *cancel culture* and you have more divisiveness, more blame and more all-or-nothing solutions. If you don't agree with me, you're canceled.

At the same time, social media, 24/7 news, and many leaders have come to embrace what we call *blamespeak*. It's a denial of responsibility and an increasingly routine pattern of impulsively attacking others with little thought or empathy or concern about solving real problems. Yet understanding blamespeak can help you overcome it, even when you *feel* like responding with more blamespeak yourself. There is a better way: BIFF communications are Brief, Informative, Friendly and Firm. But before we explain how this method works, we want to take a quick look at why blamespeak can hook you in so quickly and easily, and what *not* to do in response.

## Attack-Defend-Attack

Suppose someone says to you: "This report you prepared is worthless! The recommendations and the supporting data don't fit together at all. I can't believe they allow you to work for us."

How would you feel? Pretty rotten. What's important to realize here is that this blamespeak is NOT about you! It's about the person throwing blamespeak at you. They lack the skills to control their impulses. They lack self-awareness of how their blamespeak impacts other people. And they lack true skills of solving problems, which aren't about blame at all but rather about analyzing the dynamics of problems and searching for solutions.

The recommendations and the data don't fit? Then let's see where the problem is. Very few of today's problems are all one person's fault. But why is it so easy to get defensive? We often feel compelled to defend ourselves in a never-ending downward spiral of attack-defend-attack.

## *Why* Blamespeak Can Hook You

Our brains have two basic response systems to problems: defensive reacting and logical problem-solving. While brain researchers have many different theories of why and how this works, we like the theory that it has a lot to do with the left brain being more logical and the right brain managing more of the reacting, among other things. While right brain and left brain thinking fell out of favor as too simplistic years ago, these days there is recognition that there are some ways in which they think differently and that understanding this can be helpful.

It appears that the right hemisphere of the brain is where more of our negative emotions and defensive reactions are processed and that this can occur very quickly (less than a tenth of a second) and unconsciously. We see or hear a threat, and we are reacting even before we realize it. On the other hand, the left hemisphere of the brain is where language and logical problem-solving are primarily processed, with slightly more time to think consciously and analytically while searching for solutions. (Schore, 2019)

The result of this is that you can get emotionally hooked by what someone says or writes to you before you even realize it. Then, your response may automatically be protective: "I have to fight back to defend myself," your brain may decide, even before you have consciously absorbed what was said. However, you can train your brain to respond differently.

## *You* Can be a Conflict Influencer

Our brains are constantly growing new neurons and new connections between neurons to create new pathways for responding to situations. Just like athletes and musicians practice to strengthen their skills, we can all practice to change our responses—even when hostility or misinformation is directed at us!

What this means is that we can *choose* whether to respond to hostility and misinformation with a fight, flight or freeze response, or we can *choose* to respond with logic and information. If we can shift ourselves—essentially from defensiveness to problem-solving—then we can communicate more logically and possibly shift the other person. This is the fundamental intent of BIFF communications.

It's all about making decisions. You get to decide whether you will be a *conflict* influencer for the bad or for the good. You get to decide if you will starve or feed the conflict.

But you have to watch out for several things, otherwise you won't be able to do this.

## *How* Blamespeak Hooks Us

Blamespeak has several ways it can hook your brain into reacting defensively, triggering a fight, flight or freeze response:

1. It's usually **emotionally intense** and out of proportion to the issues. Sometimes it can seem calm but be subtle and passive aggressive and bring out the worst in a reasonable person's response. It grabs your right brain because it feels like an attack because it is an attack. It's emotional, as compared to logical problem-solving. You *feel* in danger.

2. It's **very personal**: about your intelligence, sanity, memory, ethics, sex life, looks, race, gender, and so forth.

3. It's **all your fault**: the blamespeaker feels no responsibility for the problem or the solution. That's what allows them to have their surprising intensity for blaming others.

4. It's **out of context**: it ignores all of the good you've done and all of the bad the blamespeaker has done.

5. It's often **shared with others** to emphasize how "blame-*worthy*" you are and how "blame*less*" the speaker is. The blamespeaker may have no sense of shame, embarrassment, or boundaries. He or she may speak this way about you in public. Unfortunately, blamespeak often sounds believable to those who aren't informed about your situation. If you believe that others agree with the blamespeaker, you will feel even more defensive. You will feel outnumbered.

6. You have an **intensely negative gut feeling** about the blamespeak, which sickens you, makes you feel intensely fearful, suddenly helpless, and/or very angry at someone: the blamespeaker or another one of their targets of blame.

7. You feel **compelled to respond with blamespeak** of your own. It is extremely hard to step back to prepare a reasonable response, or to decide not to respond at all.

You can easily see why someone might react defensively when confronted with blamespeak. Most people don't use blamespeak very often, if at all. But some people use it a lot. Beware.

## High Conflict People

We think of people who regularly increase the intensity of conflicts or prolong conflicts as high conflict people or HCPs. They frequently use blamespeak. They tend to have four primary characteristics:

1. Preoccupation with blaming others (without taking responsibility themselves)
2. Lots of all-or-nothing thinking (and all-or-nothing solutions to problems)
3. Unmanaged or intense emotions (which can completely take over)
4. Extreme behavior or threats (which 90% of people would never do)

They also may have a personality disorder or traits of such a disorder. These disorders are beyond the scope of this book, but understanding their high conflict behavior is enough to help you know how to focus.

| **4**<br>PRIMARY TRAITS<br>of the High Conflict<br>Personality | BLAMING OTHERS<br>preoccupied with focusing on a Target of Blame | ALL-OR-NOTHING<br>problem-solving dominated by all-or-nothing thinking | UNMANAGED EMOTIONS<br>which are intense and can completely take over | EXTREME BEHAVIOR<br>or threats, which 90% of people would never do |
|---|---|---|---|---|

[**Important note:** Don't ever tell someone you think they are a high conflict person or have a personality disorder, or they will make your life miserable for weeks or months or years. Besides, you might not be right. Instead, it's better to stay calm and use the methods in this book and other books about HCPs at our website, if you wish: www.highconflictinstitute.com.]

Many HCPs may be stuck in their defensive reacting brain or switch back and forth from surprisingly friendly to surprisingly blaming in a matter of seconds. This may be because such behavior was tolerated or encouraged while they were growing up, or because of genetic tendencies or abuse as a child. (Teicher, 2002)

HCPs at work can be customers, co-workers, managers, and even business owners. They are in every occupation, geographic area, culture, race and level of intelligence. There's no barrier to entry; it's equal opportunity. Today's culture of blame and disrespect tends to encourage and reinforce blamespeak, so they often have no shame about their blaming behavior. In fact, many see it as a badge of honor and take it to a gamesmanship level. Many believe they have to act this way because the world's a jungle or someone else treated them badly (perhaps just in their perception). They are constantly justifying their actions rather than reflecting on them and attempting to change.

It may take a while to realize that someone is an HCP, as they can behave very well at times, especially in public. They usually show their worst behavior in close relationships or under stress. Over time you may see a pattern or there may be a single behavior that 90% of people would never do. This is because they have gotten used to extreme behavior, which supports even more extreme behavior.

Regardless of whether you are communicating with an HCP or ordinary person at work (or any situation), you can use

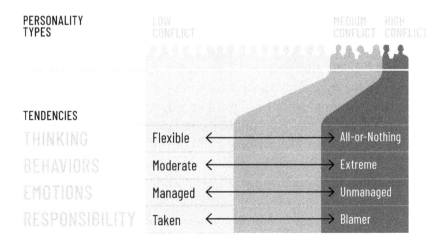

| PERSONALITY TYPES | LOW CONFLICT | | MEDIUM CONFLICT | HIGH CONFLICT |
|---|---|---|---|---|
| **TENDENCIES** | | | | |
| THINKING | Flexible | ← → | All-or-Nothing | |
| BEHAVIORS | Moderate | ← → | Extreme | |
| EMOTIONS | Managed | ← → | Unmanaged | |
| RESPONSIBILITY | Taken | ← → | Blamer | |

the BIFF communication method with them. You will just need to be more careful and more persistent if you suspect the other person is an HCP.

## The 4 Fuhgedaboudits

Because of their defensiveness, we have learned that its best to avoid the following four things with HCPs:

1 **Forget about trying to give them insight into themselves.** This is because they are highly defensive and interpret any feedback about their behavior—no matter how well-intentioned—to be a hostile attack. It may be that they are mostly thinking with their right brain defensiveness, so that insight (a primarily left brain activity) just won't occur.

2 **Forget about focusing on the past.** Focus on what to do now and in the future instead. This is because they have been getting negative feedback about their behavior all their lives and they aren't going to change now. You may need to talk about some past problem but focus most of your attention and information on current and future solutions.

3 **Forget about opening up emotions.** High conflict people tend to carry a lot of unresolved upset emotions around with them. Also, their ways of interacting with people generally don't work, so they are constantly feeling frustrated, helpless, vulnerable, weak and like a victim-in-life. If you ask how they are feeling, they will usually tell you that they feel awful—and then focus their anger on you. It's better to stay focused on thinking and doing—thinking of solutions and doing what needs to be done next.

4 **Forget about labeling them.** Avoid calling them a high conflict person or any other unnecessary name. Many people have done that in an effort to motivate them or shame them into better behavior, but it never works and worsens your relationship with them. Stay focused on choices and thinking and doing.

BIFF communications will help you avoid doing these things. You don't need to figure out whether someone is an HCP or not, to steer clear of these four Fuhgedaboudits. You can apply these principles to any conflict resolution situation. If you do not avoid these four things, you will likely get a blast of blamespeak on a regular basis. No one wants that.

## Conclusion

Our brains tend to have two types of responses to problems. When others treat us with hostility or provide misinformation, it's easy for us to get hooked into reacting defensively. However, if we can train ourselves to respond to such behavior with calm information, we will be better able to defuse the hostility and possibly correct the misinformation in most situations. But we have to watch out for emotional triggers.

Blamespeak is a common and increasing problem in to-day's workplace. It is all about giving up responsibility and not about real problem-solving. Some people are stuck in a pattern of blamespeak, who we think of as high conflict people (HCPs), but don't tell them that. There are several things to avoid in BIFF communications, including the 4 Fuhgedaboudits. The tools for using BIFF communications instead are contained in the rest of this book.

## CHAPTER 2

# How to Write a BIFF Communication

BIFF communications are:

**B**RIEF
**I**NFORMATIVE
**F**RIENDLY
**F**IRM

They help you focus on what is important and leave everything else out. They are designed to be in writing, but you can use this approach for an in-person conversation too. However, we recommend that you focus on writing good BIFF communications first, because they give you time to think before sending.

Here is the reasoning behind each of these four principles:

## BRIEF

This keeps the communication totally focused on what is necessary and nothing more. Generally, BIFF communications are a paragraph, such as 3-5 sentences. This isn't a rigid rule, but the longer the BIFF is the higher the risk of triggering or re-triggering the other person's defensiveness—especially if they are defensive much of the time. This also helps you avoid getting bogged down in writing a long explanation of why you are right and the other person is wrong. We want to steer clear of that type of interaction, which just goes downhill. Occasionally, BIFF communications may be a full page if there are important details to explain, but this should be rare. This also shouldn't be so brief that its abrupt. Sometimes people want to write a single sentence or half sentence or word. (The answer is NO!) That usually backfires and escalates the conflict rather than calming it.

## INFORMATIVE

It should provide straight information related to the issue at hand. It should not be emotional, judgmental, opinionated, defensive, or criticizing. Just straight information. Since it should be brief, this information could be contained in a sentence or two in most cases. Ideally, the information is logical information, such as what time something occurred or occurs; where something may take place; and how a task may be done. It may help to start a sentence with: "For your information…" This keeps it focused on the actual information that needs to be conveyed. In a sense, you want to appeal to their left brain problem-solving thinking, rather than to their right brain defensive reactions. This is where you decide how they will respond to you, if at all. Straight information often ends the need for further discussion.

## FRIENDLY

This may seem like the last thing you want to do, but it sets the tone for calming a hostile interaction and keeps it from escalating. Friendly can be brief, such as a friendly greeting: "Thanks for responding." Or: "Thanks for your information." Or: "Thanks for considering my request." That's often all you need to write to set the tone as a calming one, rather than inciting a strong negative reaction. It doesn't have to be super-friendly. In some cases, you might add a friendly closing, if it seems appropriate. If it's Friday afternoon, you might say: "Have a good weekend." If it really doesn't seem to fit the situation, just make sure that your BIFF does not have an unfriendly tone. Just be matter-of-fact if you think a friendly phrase would backfire. But from our experience, you can usually think of something at least mildly friendly.

## FIRM

The idea here is to end any hostility or clear up any misinformation. This doesn't mean harsh. It may mean setting limits on what you will or won't do, in a matter-of-fact way stated with a friendly tone. You don't want to put out any hooks that will feed another hostile response. Your BIFF should just end the matter and they often do. In many cases, people don't get a further response after a well-formed BIFF. However, in some cases, you may need an answer to a question. If so, we encourage you to boil it down to a Yes or No answer, and say something like: "With this information, I hope you will approve our proposal. Please let me know by Thursday at 5pm, Yes or No." Keep it simple, but with a deadline. If you are dealing with a high conflict person, they often won't respond unless there is a date and time given.

## BIFF Communications

That's it! That's all there is to a BIFF communication. While they were originally designed as a "BIFF response" to hostile or misinformed emails and texts, BIFF can also be used to start a written conversation. That's why we talk about BIFF communications now more than just BIFF responses. Perhaps you need to write an official letter on behalf of your organization to an individual or another organization and you fear that they will react negatively. If you write it as a BIFF, it improves your chances of a reasonable and respectful response to whatever you initiate.

But most of your BIFFs will be BIFF responses, because you are responding to an attack or serious misinformation in a communication you received.

# B I F F

## BRIEF

Focus on what **is necessary** and nothing more

Keep it to **3-5 sentences** as a general rule
a longer response increases the risk of triggering defensiveness

**Avoid** being too brief
to not come across as abrupt

**Avoid** giving insight
it will trigger defensiveness about why they are right/you are wrong

## INFORMATIVE

Provide **straight information** related to the issue at hand

**Refrain** from being emotional
judgmental, opinionated, defensive, and/or critical

Give **logical** information
what, when, where, how...

Appeal to **problem-solving** thinking
their left brain

**Avoid** defensive reactions
by triggering their right brain

## FRIENDLY

**Set the tone** for calming a hostile interaction

GREETING EXAMPLES
*"**Thanks** for responding"*

*"**Thanks** for the information"*

Keep things **matter-of-fact**
You don't have to be overtly friendly

CLOSING EXAMPLES
*"Have a good evening/weekend"*

*"Thanks for your help"*

## FIRM

**End** hostility or **clear up** misinformation
Firm doesn't mean harsh

**Set limits** to end the matter

Boil it down to a **Yes or No** question
If an answer is needed

EXAMPLE
*"With this information, I hope you will approve our proposal. Please let me know by Thursday at 5pm, Yes or No"*

## Customer Service Example

**Kelly's email to TV store:**

> Dear Fred's TV,
>
> I just received my flat screen TV that I purchased from you and was delivered today. IT DOESN'T WORK!!! It just shows a black screen when it's off and a blank blue screen when it's turned on, with NOTHING HAPPENING. I called my cable service and they say it's all your fault. The TV must be broken or never worked. I CAN'T HAVE THIS!!! My daughter is supposed to be watching certain programs for her schoolwork and SHE WILL FAIL if you don't fix this situation right away! Please send someone to my house with a new TV immediately!!! Or else I will tell everyone I know how faulty your products are or how incompetent your employees are—or BOTH!!! Call me about when they will be arriving with the new TV.
>
> Kelly Rager   555-888-9999

If you worked for the customer service department for Fred's TV store, would this be a BIFF communication?

> Dear Kelly,
>
> Calm down. There's no need to be so upset. When the TV just turns blue like that, it is a sign of something that needs adjusting. I have forwarded your email to our service department and someone will be calling you shortly. And there's no need to threaten our products or our staff. I'm sorry, but we have excellent products and an excellent team.
>
> Caren Calm

**Was this a BIFF?**

**Was this Brief?** Yes, it was just a paragraph.

**Was this Informative?** Yes, BUT it also included some defensive words about products and staff.

**Was this Friendly?** Not really. Telling someone to calm down is usually interpreted as condescending. There were no friendly words at the beginning or end.

**Was this Firm?** Not really. By criticizing her for being upset and for her threat about telling others, Caren has opened the door to a back and forth as Kelly will feel that she needs to defend herself against a perceived attack from Caren.
**This was not a BIFF response.**

**Let's try again. Is this a BIFF?**

> Dear Kelly,
>
> That sounds so frustrating. These new-fangled products can be so confusing. When the TV just turns blue like that, it is sometimes a sign of something that needs adjusting. I have forwarded your email to our service department and someone will be calling you shortly. If you don't hear from someone within the hour, please contact me again at this email address. Thank you for giving us your phone number.
>
> Caren Calm

**Was this Brief?** Yes. Just a paragraph.

**Informative?** Yes. Sometimes it just needs adjusting, but she's not saying that absolutely. She wants to be realistic and not blame Kelly for misunderstanding their product. Someone will call.

**Friendly?** Yes. She empathizes with her: That's frustrating. It can be confusing. Thanks for your number.

**Firm**? Yes. She has clearly taken care of the situation for now. You'll note that there was no reason to admonish Kelly to calm down or to stop making threats. If Kelly gets a good BIFF response, she won't be thinking like this anymore.

This is a good BIFF response.

## More Than One Right Way

There's more than one right way to write a BIFF. It depends on three factors:

- Who the BIFF writer is.
- Who the BIFF reader is.
- What the situation is.

To demonstrate this using the sample above, here are some possible variations:

*The BIFF Writer:* A different Customer Service Rep might not be allowed to have called her back, so they would leave that part out. Depending on their style, a different BIFF writer might not include the sentence about "new-fangled" products.

*The BIFF Reader:* Perhaps Kelly has made similar complaints before about other products, in which case it might be shorter this time in order to avoid encouraging her to communicate.

*The Situation:* There may be a booklet that came with the TV that explains how to turn it on. In that case, a knowledgeable Customer Service Rep might guide Kelly to the booklet instead of referring her to another person.

As long as its Brief, Informative, Friendly and Firm, it should be a BIFF communication.

## Avoid the Three A's

In addition to checking to see if a communication is brief, informative, friendly and firm, it helps to check it for any of the Three A's: advice, admonishments, and apologies. Here's why:

**1. Advice:** When someone writes you an angry email, text or otherwise, they are *not* usually asking for your advice. They are trying to give you *their* advice. They are trying to put you down with their upset. If you try to put them down in return, you will simply trigger an escalation of anger and difficulty. Instead, just give them straight information.

This is a common problem between older and younger employees, and experienced and inexperienced employees. Just try to address the issue at hand without calling it "advice." That feels demeaning to people who are already feeling upset. Don't write this: "Let me give you some advice buddy, THIS is how you remove the crank to repair the cylinder..." Instead, just write this: "This is how you can remove the crank to repair the cylinder..."

**2. Admonishments:** This is a more obvious example of trying to put down the person who sent you an angry or misinformed communication. Parents admonish their children. Judges admonish people in court. In a work relationship, no one likes to be admonished, whether they are a customer, an employee, or a manager, especially if they are already upset. You'll be better off if you keep such language out of any BIFF communications.

**3. Apologies:** This is the most surprising thing about BIFF communications. It is the opposite of what you would think. In most situations, apologies are a good thing and work well at calming conflicts. But when you are responding to a high conflict person or someone who is already angry at you, they tend to have all-or-nothing thinking. This means that if you apologize for something small, they hear that you agree that the whole situation or relationship is all your fault.

We have witnessed bullies carrying around notes in which someone tried to calm them down by apologizing to them for something small. ("Hey Sam: Sorry I didn't clean up after myself in the lunchroom yesterday.") But instead, the bully has used it to tell the world that the note-writer was the one completely at fault for a wide range of issues (because of their all-or-nothing thinking) and they hold the note up as proof. So, we recommend that you do not apologize in BIFF communications. Just provide the information that's needed.

If you want to explain the situation without an apology, you could just say the facts without the apology. ("Hey Sam: I had a sudden important call and didn't clean up after myself in the lunchroom yesterday, if you're wondering who it was. That shouldn't happen again.")

What about social apologies? This is a good question. We often say things like: "Sorry, I was five minutes late to the meeting yesterday." Or: "I'm sorry to see you're in this difficult situation." These might not get you into trouble, but in some situations (especially with particularly high conflict people) you might want to avoid even saying the word "sorry" at all. In that case, you can just leave off the "sorry": "I know, I was five minutes late to the meeting yesterday." Or: "I'm saddened to see you're in this difficult situation." Replacing "sorry" with "saddened" works well in many situations.

Checking your BIFF communications for the Three A's will save you a lot of grief in the long run. You can also keep these principles in mind regarding any interactions with potentially high conflict people. When in doubt, leave it out!

Back to our customer service rep situation above, can you quickly see why Caren's first response was not a BIFF?

Dear Kelly,

Calm down. There's no need to be so upset. When the TV just turns blue like that, it is a sign of something that needs adjusting. I have forwarded your email to our service department and someone will be calling you shortly. And there's no need to threaten our products or our staff. I'm sorry, but we have excellent products and an excellent team.

Caren Calm

You're right, if you identified these phrases as:

**Admonishments:** "Calm down. There's no need to be so upset."

**Apologies:** "I'm sorry, but…"

*But many employees are taught to apologize!* This is a common approach for many businesses. Apologize to calm down the customers, and it often works. However, when you are dealing with HCPs, you run some risks of inviting more anger at you and your company, not less. These simple tips can help you avoid reinforcing the customer's upset feelings by directing attention to simple information in a friendly (but unapologetic) BIFF communication. Of course, follow your company's policies if they have a required manner of responding, or encourage them to upgrade their policy with BIFF in mind.

AVOID THE

# 3 A's

ADVICE

ADMONISHMENTS

APOLOGIES

## Conclusion

It's fairly easy to write a BIFF communication, especially when you get used to breaking it down into these simple steps. The easiest way to learn this method is to write out a response to a hostile or misinformed communication, then check it for being Brief, Informative, Friendly, and Firm. Then, check it for any Advice, Admonishments, or Apologies. It's actually harder than it sounds at first, but it gets easier with practice. The rest of this book will give you many practice opportunities.

We also recommend that you get your BIFF communications checked by a co-worker or friend before sending them out. Sometimes they will catch something that you missed in looking at your own words over and over again. In the last section of this book, we will teach you a coaching method to help someone else with their BIFF communications and for others to help you with yours. A BIFF buddy, if you will.

## CHAPTER 3

# When to Use BIFF

BIFFs can be used when you need to respond to a hostile communication, but they're also helpful when initiating an email, text or letter to someone who won't take it well—possibly (likely) someone with a high conflict personality. Most people have been in both situations and often dread it.

When you are nervous about initiating a written communication, taking time to use the BIFF structure may prevent threats of (or actual) legal action, licensure complaints, harassment allegations, EO complaints, or time tied up in meetings in HR. You have nothing to lose by using BIFF. Ask yourself the opportunity cost of not using it.

Do you need to respond? People often ignore hostile or misinformed written communications. They don't want to reward an unnecessary comment with attention, or they figure that other people who saw it will realize it is absurd or obviously untrue. Sometimes it makes sense not to respond. However, we have found that it may be better to respond with a BIFF communication in many situations. You can address misinformation and set limits on further hostility. If other people are involved, there is often someone who will believe an absurd statement if it appears that you agree with it by your silence. Here is a way to think about whether to respond or not.

## Should You Respond Individually?

There are several considerations.

*Are you trying to change a high conflict person's mind?* If it is just a correspondence between you and another individual, and you are trying to change their mind, you might just forget about it. That would be a pointless effort at trying to give them insight. (See 4 Fuhgedaboudits in Chapter 1.) It may not be worth responding to.

*Have you already sent a BIFF response?* It's not unusual after you have given a BIFF communication that the other person replies to that in a challenging way. Do you keep responding? If you have said all you need to say on the issue, you could simply not respond or you could write a briefer BIFF and say that you will not be responding further on this topic because you have already said all that you are going to say about it in your prior email of such-and-such date. Then, if they reply again, you don't need to respond any further since you already told them you were done.

*Did it go out to other people?* HCPs often like to draw lots of others into their conflicts, such as by copying your whole workgroup or the president of the company in their complaint about you. In this case, it is usually wise to respond and copy the same group that was drawn into this, so that they know it is being taken care of and they don't need to get involved. Most people don't want to get involved in other people's conflicts, unless they feel it's necessary. Here is one way you can do that:

## Colleagues Were Copied Example

Dear Colleagues:

You have been copied on an email to me regarding a private, internal matter in our division. There is no reason that you need to get involved or concern yourself with this at all. The issues raised are not at all agreed upon and are being appropriately discussed within normal procedures. If you have any questions or concerns for me about this, please feel free to contact me at any time.

Best wishes.

This BIFF simply and briefly lets others know that you do not agree with the information that they were copied on, so that it doesn't become assumed to be true by anyone. It reassures people that it's a private matter, so they don't need to get involved even though they were copied on the correspondence. It also makes clear that you do not feel defensive about its content, since you are open to people asking you questions.

In most situations, when others know they can contact you to discuss something like this, they really don't want to know any more about it. This settles the matter. It's informative without going into any details, because the door is open for anyone who wants to get information. That usually ends the matter. All together it is Brief, Informative, Friendly and Firm.

*Is it potentially part of a legal case?* Emails, texts, and other correspondence can easily end up in a court case these days. Even if there isn't a legal case going, you may want to prepare your response as though it could end up in court. (If there is a court case, it can be illegal to destroy electronically stored information.) In court, BIFF communications sure look better than the hostile communications you may have received in the first place.

If the other person is saying that you were irresponsible and didn't handle your duties well, you will need to respond and explain why this is not true (if it isn't), or how you are dealing with it (if it is true). Unanswered allegations often gain attention and strength in today's culture of blame and disrespect. If their correspondence is filed with the court, you will want yours to be too. Don't let allegations go unanswered and don't wait too long. Of course, make sure you have plenty of legal advice on how to respond.

Most BIFF communications can be a paragraph even if it is in response to a long-winded, blaming email or other correspondence. However, an exception to this guideline is legal matters. You may need to respond to each item or allegation made against you, even if it is just in email or letter form at the time. These things can grow when they are not responded to. If the other person suddenly files their correspondence with a court or human resources or some other authority, you want your response to have been already sent or at least prepared at the time when it was fresh. Again, get legal advice on your responses to potentially legal allegations.

## Should You Respond Organizationally?

Most businesses, large and small, are getting attacked with blamespeak these days. We recommend putting out BIFF responses rather than ignoring some of this. One of the best examples of this was how a pizza company dealt with a public relations crisis several years ago. We described this in our first BIFF book as follows:

## Pizza Company Example

A few years ago two pizza employees made a video of themselves sticking cheese up their noses and putting it on food they were preparing to deliver, and other pranks. It went viral and lots of people had a big laugh. I don't know whether the two employees were HCPs, but there were reports that one had a criminal history (which might indicate a *pattern* of high-conflict behavior), and they certainly had very bad judgment that affected the whole business. Did they think that people would believe that they were actually doing this, or just faking it? Apparently, they were truly surprised when their employer found out!

Many people lost their faith in the company and sales started to plummet. The pizza company realized how important it was to provide a quick response. They developed and implemented a social media campaign and posted a video on YouTube featuring the company president that was just under two minutes, including the following statements:

"This was an isolated incident… There is nothing more important or sacred to us than our customers trust… It sickens me that the acts of two individuals could impact our great system."

**Is it a BIFF?**

**Brief?** Yes. It was just under two minutes and probably the perfect length for addressing this problem to the public.

**Informative?** Yes. It explained the actions the company was taking to clean up the store, to tighten hiring procedures and to immediately fire and bring legal action against the two employees. The focus was the key points above: that it was an isolated incident, their customers are "sacred" to them and that they are still a great company.

**Friendly?** Yes, toward their customers. It was understandable that they were not friendly toward the two fired employees, but they didn't get stuck on blasting them – they kept the focus on what the company was doing.

**Firm?** Yes. They made it clear that the problem was small and had been resolved.

This is a good example of taking a rumor seriously and giving a quick response. Apparently, the company totally recovered. It demonstrates the importance of quick BIFFs in today's interconnected world for any business, organization or individual. *(Eddy, 2014, 123-124)*

## BIFF as Risk & Reputation Management

**Risk Management**

BIFF communications may help your organization avoid a lawsuit or complaint. The following is an example of how Bill responded to a threatened lawsuit. While such a lawsuit would not have gotten very far, the time and stress involved of responding can be overwhelming—even though these types of lawsuits rarely succeed.

When Bill stopped representing clients in family court and switched to mediation, consultation and training, he left the names of several lawyers he recommended for family law practice on his Law Office website. One day he received the following email:

## Lawsuit Was Threatened Example

August 1st: From: Joe Jones (not his real name)

Greetings Mr. Eddy:

I'd like to thank you for all the resources you've made available on your website. Because I had found so much helpful information on your site in the past I was very willing to call one of the attorneys you endorse. Unfortunately Ms. Smith (in my opinion) doesn't seem very well versed in even divorce let alone high conflict divorce. I'm no legal expert but it seems Ms. Smith is significantly lacking in her skill set….

[2 long pages blaming Ms. Smith]

I mean….what has she done …? Nothing… Absolutely Nothing…. How is this behavior, that which you endorse on your website, a reflection of an attorney that's even responsive to the situation let alone one well versed in high conflict divorce. **As my decision to hire Ms. Smith was based solely on your recommendation and**

**promotion, I intend to file suit against you** unless you cease all promotion of Ms. Smith on your website. I look forward to your response by August 4th.

Just think about it…I'm supposed see my kids today…. but I don't get to because my wife ignores court orders and my attorney does NOTHING…. I'M LOSING MY FAMILY BECAUSE MY ATTORNEY DOES NOTHING!! And you promote her on your website….. THANKS EVERYONE…GREAT JOB.

After writing out a draft and getting some coaching from a colleague, here is the BIFF response Bill sent. It is longer than he usually would write, but he believed that he needed to give more useful information in this case.

Monday, Aug. 4

Hi Joe,

Thanks for your positive feedback on my website. I'm glad that it has been helpful to you.

I was saddened to read that your divorce has been so difficult. I was also disappointed to read that your relationship with your attorney is not working out. I have not had other complaints about Ms. Smith, but some clients and professionals fit together better than others. That is why I always recommend interviewing several. Once there are strong criticisms made it is unlikely you can work together in the future, so it makes sense to look elsewhere.

There are several factors which influence a case. Regarding denial of visitation in a high conflict case, a general principle of mine is to consider several potential options such as asking for a Parenting Coordinator, requesting some form of family counseling, and documenting specific problems in writing to present to the court at a hearing. Of course, these are general principles since I cannot give you advice for your specific case. I would encourage you to discuss these ideas with a new attorney as soon as possible.

Best wishes,
Bill

Here is the response that Bill received that same day:

Monday, Aug. 4

Hello Mr. Eddy,

Thank you for taking the time to respond. I suppose if Ms. Smith had responded to my e-mail(s) a month ago none of this "back and forth" would have occurred. As my advocate I thought Ms. Smith would have taken some action when my wife repeatedly ignored visitation orders however Ms. Smith chose instead to ignore me…. [**1 long page blaming Ms. Smith**]

Anyway, I'm obviously lost and in a lot of emotional discomfort. Thanks again for responding. I appreciate the thoughtfulness of your e-mail and I won't bother you again.

Kindest Regards,

Joe Jones


Both of these examples demonstrate the importance of a response and a timely response to attacks on one's business. The pizza company responded quickly, in a manner that was Brief, Informative, Friendly and Firm. Yes, this can be applied to videos on YouTube as well as written responses. If the pizza company had not responded, it would probably be out of business today, as its stock tanked for a couple days before they responded. If Bill had not responded to Joe Jones, it's hard to say what would have happened, given that Mr. Jones would not have been successful suing him for picking a lawyer out of seven possibilities and choosing to hire her. But an upset person can create a legal nightmare for any business if they feel ignored or disrespected enough.

## Reputation Management

The risk of reputational damage ranks near or at the top of the list when it comes to impact on the business. In a study by Deloitte and Forbes Insights of 300 executives, brand reputation was considered the highest strategic risk area, for good reason. A smear to your brand can kick off a drop in revenue or an investigation by authorities, which no company wants. Time is money and you don't want to spend your time or money defending and repairing your brand's reputation.

Strong communication policies that are communicated widely throughout the organization are a reputation risk management tool, and that includes policies about email, text messages, social media posts, replies, and letters. All written communication should be under this umbrella and BIFF should be included directly in the policy document (at least we think so) along with brief BIFF training for everyone.

BIFF provides structure and boundaries, both of which are becoming more important in today's rapid fire instant communication world. We speed read through our Twitter feed and, depending on our mood or stage of current anxiety-producing hysteria (political, stock market, social justice), impulsively and instantaneously re-tweet or worse, we quickly type the first thought that enters our mind. Voilà, it's out there. Someone has already grabbed the screenshot, obfuscating deletion. A career ruined in a fraction of a second. A brand damaged. Bruised stock. Worse, in the era of cancel culture, your company might be canceled.

Learn BIFF and practice it faithfully. Set a morning reminder on your phone. It bears repeating: If you lead any size organization, teach everyone in the organization and make it policy.

## Conclusion

Biff communications are a simple and handy way of managing upset people in any setting. However, in the world of employment and business, they can really save the day. Deciding whether to use a BIFF response to hostile or misinformed communications is always an individual choice. But our experience had taught us that it is better to err on the side of a cautious BIFF response than hoping no one else will get involved or be misled. Whether there is a potential legal case or a public relations crisis, one should seriously consider using a BIFF communication. One should also make sure to get legal advice in the process.

The next section of this book addresses BIFF communications with those outside of the organization, including customers, vendors, and clients of a professional practice.

# SECTION 2

# BIFF for External Communications

.

**CHAPTER 4**

# BIFFs for Customers and Customer Service

Hell hath no fury like a customer who can't get online because their Internet is out and they can't find the company's phone number on the website because they can't get on the website. And it's not the first time it's happened.

Or the customer who watches the rental car agent take customers out of order, serving the guy behind you when it's your turn. Especially after standing in the rental car line after a long overseas flight desperate to get the car and off to an important appointment. Objections are raised but the desk agent is oblivious and continues helping the line-cutting customer.

Rest assured that the company will receive a phone call, letter or email. The unpleasant kind.

How the company responds will determine important outcomes:

- whether more company resources will be expended if the issue isn't resolved in one contact
- risk of reputational damage from public shaming, bad-mouthing
- potential revenue losses

This is why many large organizations spend millions on customer service training for employees. You know when you're dealing with a well-trained customer service agent and when you're not. Many organizations, small businesses, non-profits, and even some corporations aren't able to or choose not to make the same investment and it often shows.

When a customer inquiry comes in the form of an email, text, letter or chat, responding with BIFF can be the determining factor in those important outcomes. The good news is that anyone from any size organization can use BIFF. The ROI is extraordinarily high. The requirements? Read this book and apply it.

## Customer Service-Bookstore Example

**Delivered by Email**

> Name: Hannah Pike
> Email Address: hannahpike2@i.me
> Subject: RIP OFF PACKAGE
>
> Message: I am FURIOUS! I ordered a PACKAGE, not one damn book! I could have bought the book only from any other website for far less money! ORDER NUMBER: 602-A-329
>
> You literally charged me $57.00 for ONE paperback book. I ordered a PACKAGE for $57.00 but all that came is the ONE book!!!! I want a prepaid shipping label IMMEDIATELY and a FULL REFUND, including shipping like NOW, or I am posting this RIP OFF on social media. This is disgraceful! I have photos of your invoice showing you did charge me $57.00 PLUS $7.95 shipping for ONE DAMN BOOK! I will be contacting the author as well. He should know how your company is stealing from people.

## Response #1

Ms. Pike:

We are not a company that sells rip off packages and we believe our books are reasonably priced. We do not provide refunds as per the Terms & Conditions on our website that required agreement before you made the purchase. After you respond with the name of the book you received, we will ship the other books. Not sure if you are aware of the impact your all caps email has on the person receiving it or not. You may want to think about that in future.

Sincerely,
Adam

## BIFF CHECKER

| | |
|---|---|
| **Is a response necessary?** | **YES** |

| | |
|---|---|
| **Brief?** (2-5 sentences) | **MAYBE** |

At five sentences, it meets the criteria but five sentences are not necessary.

| | |
|---|---|
| **Informative?** (who, what, when, where, what for) | **NO** |

Adam blows it the first sentence by defending the company instead of focusing on the customer's needs. The second sentence is informational but the first sentence has already angered the customer and this sentence worded this way will only increase her anger as it places blame on her. If she makes it to the third sentence, anger again, as action is required on her part when the company was at fault.

| | |
|---|---|
| **Friendly?** | **NO** |

It is formal, not friendly, and it is defensive and demanding.

| Firm? | YES |
|---|---|
| It is firm but in the wrong way. | |

| Advice? | YES |
|---|---|
| Sentences 4-5 are nuclear and are likely to ignite the customer to put the company on blast on social media and to complain to the author. | |

| Admonishments? | YES |
|---|---|
| Sentences 4-5 are also admonishments. | |

| Apologies? | NO |
|---|---|

| IS IT A BIFF? | NO |
|---|---|

Let's try again. Is this a BIFF?

> Dear Ms. Pike,
>
> I am so sorry that we messed up your order. I imagine that was quite upsetting. We have no excuse other than human error, which we can correct immediately.
>
> We will ship the other books via Priority Mail today, which would have them to you within 2-3 days.
>
> If you prefer to have a refund, we will refund the money to your credit card and send a pre-paid shipping label and packaging to return the books.
>
> Thank you for your patience—it's much appreciated.
>
> Kind regards,
> Adam

Before we go to the BIFF Checker, stop and think about how *this* response impacted you vs. the first response. Sometimes it is palpable.

## BIFF CHECKER

| | |
|---|---|
| Is a response necessary? | **YES** |

| | |
|---|---|
| **Brief?** *(2-5 sentences)* | **YES** |

It's a little long but customer service responses sometimes require a bit more information, so in this case it's okay.

| | |
|---|---|
| **Informative?** *(who, what, when, where, what for)* | **YES** |

It describes what is being done to correct the problem.

| | |
|---|---|
| **Friendly?** | **YES** |

Signing off with "Kind regards" and thanking her for being patient. Even though she's not being patient, she will feel better thinking that Adam thinks she is. It will calm her right reactionary brain.

| | |
|---|---|
| **Firm?** | **YES** |

Firmness is demonstrated here with being decisive with action–literally being proactive instead of asking her if she prefers a refund or the books. Customers who are this upset are usually upset in that moment and have little/no option of stopping themselves before writing the email.

| | |
|---|---|
| **Advice?** | **NO** |

| | |
|---|---|
| **Admonishments?** | **NO** |

| | |
|---|---|
| **Apologies?** | **YES** |

The company made a mistake. They should apologize. The apology was followed by an EAR Statement (Empathy, Attention, Respect) that addressed her upset feelings, thereby calming the defensive brain. While we recommend against apologies in general in individual correspondence, when it's the organization involved it can be important to apologize for the sake of public relations.

## IS IT A BIFF?　　　　　　　　　　　　**YES**

## Customer Service-Power Company Example

### Inquiry Delivered via Social Media

From: Sylvia Smith
To: The Power Company

I am extremely tired of having issues with my power because you fail to trim the trees! Either cut them or I'll call an attorney! I have a father-in-law living here who survives on oxygen—which obviously requires POWER—which is your ONLY job. We are forced to spend money on spare tanks. Are you going to reimburse us for those? Get your crap together!

### Response #1

Dear Power Customer,

As you know, power companies must deal with many natural problems which can occasionally impact customer service, including storms, grid overload, and tree growth. It is unfortunate that your power was impacted by tree growth and that is why we advise our customers to report such problems to us. We have cut the tree limbs and your power was restored.

We do not reimburse for private energy-generating tanks, as that is the customer's responsibility. We are a large utility and cannot serve individuals in every household other than providing lines and power to the house. As we have written in our notice for service, power may be interrupted at times and we will not be liable for that as it is an expected consequence of living with nature.

## BIFF CHECKER

Is a response necessary?                    YES

| | |
|---|---|
| **Brief?** *(2-5 sentences)* | **MAYBE** |
| It feels a little long-winded and repetitive. | |
| **Informative?** *(who, what, when, where, what for)* | **YES** |
| It says they are not reimbursing and says why. | |
| **Friendly?** | **NO** |
| It emphasizes that they are big and you are small. | |
| **Firm?** | **YES** |
| It ends the conversation as it says you're not getting paid. | |
| **Advice?** | **MAYBE** |
| It says "we advise our clients" but it's really more information and doesn't have the negative tone of advice. | |
| **Admonishments?** | **MAYBE** |
| An "expected consequence of living with nature" could feel like an admonishment, implying the person isn't smart enough to realize that. | |
| **Apologies?** | **NO** |

## IS IT A BIFF?                        NO

**Response #2**

Dear Ms. Smith:

I can understand how worrisome that must have been, given your father-in-law's needs. I am glad you have acquired your own energy-generating tank for the rare times that our service may be interrupted without warning. Our policy does not allow us to reimburse for individual household needs, given that we have so many customers and that we warn that natural events such as tree growth do occur and that interruptions may occur without warning. Thank you for notifying us of the tree problem, which I understand we resolved last week.

Best wishes,
Fred Jones, Customer Service

## BIFF CHECKER

| | |
|---|---|
| Is a response necessary? | YES |
| Brief? *(2-5 sentences)* <br> To the point. | YES |
| Informative? *(who, what, when, where, what for)* <br> It informs about the policy that allows no reimbursements. | YES |
| Friendly? <br> The first sentence shows empathy. The second praises her for doing what should be done. The fourth emphasizes that the issue has been resolved. | YES |
| Firm? <br> It ends the conversation with a clear answer. | YES |
| Advice? | NO |
| Admonishments? | NO |
| Apologies? | NO |

## IS IT A BIFF?   YES

**Tone**
Tone makes all the difference in the world in a response to an upset customer. The second try at BIFF above shows empathy right from the start, then explains the reality of service interruptions, then informs about the policy that requires them not to reimburse. By referring to a policy, it doesn't feel like a personal rejection. By being brief, it doesn't invite a further

response and should close the case. By starting out friendly, it sets the tone to try to calm the conflict rather than escalating it.

## Customer Service – Airline Example

### Inquiry Delivered Through Company's Contact Page

To Whom It May Concern:

My family has experienced a travesty at the hands of your company. My father, who lives in Europe, passed away in March. I immediately booked a ticket (paying an exorbitant amount) to attend his funeral and bring his ashes home. Guess what? **The flight was oversold!** I got bumped. I begged the gate agents to let me on but they ignored me and told me I'd have to get online to book another flight. There were no other flights that would get me there in time. **I missed my father's funeral.** Let me repeat—I missed my father's funeral. Not only did I miss the single most important event in my father's life, I was utterly and entirely disrespected by your staff. I demand an apology from the CEO, a full refund, and a statement on all your social media pages about your error. The public has a right to know how incompetent and reprehensible you are!

Very, very unhappy customer,
Andrew Brown

### Response #1

Dear Mr. Brown,

I'm sorry you experienced such horrible treatment at the hands of our company. This is not who we are. Did you happen to get the name(s) of the employees who treated you this way? You should not have been bumped given the circumstances of your flight. Of course, this may have occurred because you were one of the last people to book your flight. As you may know, it is our policy to overbook flights since some customers do not show up. Since your experience is so rare for our airline, we will not be forwarding your complaint to the CEO, nor will we be apologizing on our social media.

Judy Green, Customer Service

## BIFF CHECKER

| | |
|---|---|
| **Is a response necessary?** | YES |
| **Brief?** *(2-5 sentences)*<br>To the point. | YES |
| **Informative?** *(who, what, when, where, what for)*<br>It says they are not refunding and says why. | YES |
| **Friendly?**<br>While it starts out giving empathy, it emphasizes what they will not be doing for him. It feels cold in response to a very sad situation. | NO |
| **Firm?**<br>It ends the conversation, but by criticizing the company (how horrible he was treated by us, without any investigation having occurred) and pointing out the company's overbooking policy, it draws negative attention unnecessarily to the company and may invite further criticism or even legal action. | MAYBE |
| **Advice?** | NO |
| **Admonishments?**<br>By pointing out that this is so rare, it feels like the customer is being admonished a little. | MAYBE |
| **Apologies?**<br>While an apology may be in order because this is a potential public relations problem, there has been no investigation yet. This is just a response to an initial inquiry on a contact page. Some high con- | YES |

flict people start out this aggressive, but then the facts don't fit their complaint. One needs to know more before determining whether an apology is in order and to whom.

## IS IT A BIFF?           NO

### Response #2

Dear Andrew,

What a sad situation! Please give us a good contact phone number, so that we can call you and understand what went wrong here. Please include Item #1635345 when you send your phone number, so we'll know what it's about.

We are in business to provide safe, dependable and friendly air transportation to our customers. If we fell down on the job, we would like to discuss what we can do about that. We are dedicated to having satisfied customers.

We look forward to speaking with you soon.

Judy Greene, Customer Service

## BIFF CHECKER

| Is a response necessary? | YES |
|---|---|

| Brief? *(2-5 sentences)* | YES |
|---|---|

It's appropriate to the situation. The extra two sentences that say they are in business to satisfy their customers help because it appears to be such a sad situation.

| Informative? *(who, what, when, where, what for)* | YES |
|---|---|

They want to discuss this with Andrew. This emphasizes that the company is open to getting Andrew's full information and will discuss what they can do about it. At this stage it's too early to be specific, and a phone call will be much more sensitive than just an email.

| Friendly? | YES |
|---|---|

From the start, the Customer Service representative says it is a sad situation and immediately wants the company to have more hands-on, personal contact with the customer. Also, there are the two sentences about being in business to have satisfied customers.

| Firm? | YES |
|---|---|

It's too soon to know how this should end. It may be that further inquiry finds out that what the customer says is all true and something needs to be done about employees who treat a customer so inconsiderately (ignoring him, etc.) and there should be some compensation (like a travel voucher). On the other hand, when people dramatically complain like this, they are sometimes high conflict people who have seriously distorted or even made up what happened, and should not be rewarded. That is why an investigation is necessary first and why personal contact will help either way.

| Advice? | NO |
|---|---|

| Admonishments? | NO |
|---|---|

| Apologies? | MAYBE |
|---|---|

It's too early to say we're sorry, although that may be an outcome. It also may be a situation in which the company should not apologize, after getting all the facts straight. By saying "If we fell down on the job, we would like to discuss what we can do about that," the door is open to a future apology which could even come from the CEO.

## IS IT A BIFF?                    YES

# Law Office Website Complaint Example

From: Jim Mendoza

Message: After many years knowing and following your website and reading your content, I see your law firm as just more of your money grab under the guise of "helping". I'm on your site now and disappointed that because I'm using the contact form on this page, I can't add other people to this email. They need to know. Since you charge a fee, do you have any referrals to anyone who will collect their fees on performance rather than your "hourly" rate? I don't want the same old excuse that you can't give free "legal" advice, which to me seems like a way to avoid providing "actual" solutions. You and your entire industry continue harming and then just deny, deny, deny and collect, collect, collect $$$.

**Response #1**

Mr. Mendoza:

I'm so sorry to know that you feel this way about our law firm and I hope you will reconsider your assessment. All of us work extraordinarily hard to provide a lot of helpful information and services at reasonable rates to anyone who visits our site (free) or calls our office (fee for service). As a business, we have to keep our doors open somehow and therefore we charge for our services. While we wish we could help everyone for free, it's simply not realistic and I truly hope you can understand this. We do "help" people. We do provide "actual" solutions. We do not give excuses. We do not harm, deny and collect $$$.

I don't know what profession you work in, but let me ask you this: do you charge a fee for your services? I imagine you get paid for the work you do. Are you beginning to see where I'm going with this? I hope this gives you some insight into where we're coming from.

As to the contact form on the site, we are bound by the platform on which our website is built; therefore, it does not have the capability of copying in other people.

Please let me know if you have additional questions.

Sincerely,
Janna Walker

## BIFF CHECKER

**Is a response necessary?**          **YES**

Public relations are important for every business. This could be a potential client.

---

**Brief?** *(2-5 sentences)*          **NO**

It goes too long and gives more than enough to irritate an angry potential client.

---

**Informative?** *(who, what, when, where, what for)*      **YES**

It explains how the business needs to charge for services to stay in business. But it also goes into justifying and defending, which often feeds more conflict.

---

**Friendly?**          **YES**

It makes an effort: "I hope you reconsider…." "I hope this gives you some insight…."

---

**Firm?**          **MAYBE**

By encouraging more questions at the end, it risks another angry response.

---

**Advice?**          **NO**

Not really

---

**Admonishments?**                              MAYBE

It feels a bit like an admonishment to explain and then say "I hope this gives you some insight…" as if the person wasn't seeing the obvious before.

---

**Apologies?**                                  MAYBE

It starts with "I'm so sorry you feel this way…" While that isn't really an apology, it sounds like one because of the "sorry." It's better not to use that word at all, so that it doesn't imply an apology that isn't necessary and doesn't irritate a potential client because it sounds like an empty apology.

---

## IS IT A BIFF?                                NO

**Response #2**

Hello Mr. Mendoza,

Thank you for your inquiry. We are a firm that provides legal services at reasonable rates. We have free educational articles on our website, but no free services and do not make referrals.

Sincerely,
Janna Walker

## BIFF CHECKER

---

**Is a response necessary?**                    YES

For good public relations and for a potential client.

---

**Brief?** *(2-5 sentences)*                    YES

This is brief and to the point.

---

**Informative?** *(who, what, when, where, what for)*    YES

This clarifies the potential client's questions and explains that there are free articles but no free services.

| Friendly? | YES |
|---|---|

There is a thank you opening and a "Best Wishes" closing.

| Firm? | YES |
|---|---|

It leaves no opening for further complaining as it fully answers what the potential client was looking for.

| Advice? | NO |
|---|---|

| Admonishments? | NO |
|---|---|

| Apologies? | NO |
|---|---|

| IS IT A BIFF? | YES |
|---|---|

This is a clear and simple BIFF Response.

## Conclusion

Customer service can use BIFF communications to respond to many complaint situations that truly can be brief, so long as they are also informative, friendly and firm. While we have given written examples here, this approach can also be used in verbal customer service responses.

Customer service is also where many high conflict people go to complain these days. Company representatives must be careful to calm the situation while not being overly abrupt and insensitive (to save time, which can feed the anger of an upset customer) or being overly apologetic (which can feed the blaming behavior of an HCP). BIFF communications help balance this increasing concern.

**CHAPTER 5**

# BIFFs for Ombuds

Whether or not someone is an ombuds, they can use the following principles in analyzing their BIFF communications. By definition, ombuds (also known as ombudsman or ombudsperson) are complaint handlers. More common in some countries than others, ombuds provide dispute resolution services between consumers and public services or companies; between citizens and government agencies; within universities for students, staff, and faculty; and in other settings.

They serve as neutral arbiters to resolve complaints and conflicts, and investigate when necessary. They offer objectivity to citizens who complain when they believe a company, organization or government has treated them unfairly.

Ombuds are independent, free and impartial, so they don't take sides. In many cases, they don't resolve the disputes, instead they guide the parties to find their own solutions or to where to get more assistance. In short, they often handle big problems with little authority. This can make dealing with high conflict people particularly challenging, since they bring complaints so often.

While some complaints are handled by phone or in person, many are received via email or by letter. While many may contain valid complaints, some are replete with unrealistic but highly contentious, blaming and demanding accusations. Ombuds don't have the option of refusing to respond, unless serious threats are made, so they have the difficult job of dealing with some of the most difficult people without the necessary benefit of setting limits on the number of contacts and complaints.

Because of their blaming nature, HCPs are drawn to the allure of the ombuds office as a place to blame, complain and get justice when they *feel wronged*. They like to get people to take their side and will use strong emotion toward this goal. This emotional power must be managed and separated from determining what has occurred and what will help resolve the dispute.

If you are in the position of handling anyone's complaints as a neutral person, be aware of your own emotions by asking yourself:

- Am I hooked by the strong emotions contained in the complaint?
- Do I feel sorry for what they're experiencing?
- Does it seem like it's all the fault of the organization?
- Do you feel a strong urge to *fix* it for the complainant?

It's extremely important to be aware of your emotions and check yourself. Start by asking the questions listed above. Like many who are drawn to the work of the ombuds, as it's the perfect place to help people in need, you may be a *fixer* by nature. It's okay if you are—you just need to be aware of that and consistently check yourself when you start feeling that *helper* pull.

After all, you don't know if the complainant's facts are truthful or not. If the writer is an HCP, the allegations may be honestly believed by them, but factually in error. They are driven by fear, which can cause them to see and believe things very differently from an ordinary upset person who is not an HCP.

So, remain objective. Stick with the structure. Write BIFF responses.

A large share of ombuds handle complaints made against

public service, e.g., government agencies, utilities, or financial services. At the same time, consumers often allege an infringement on their economic, social and cultural rights. One can imagine the human impact.

A public energy utility may fail to inform customers of a power outage on the day of a national sports championship. Fans may be livid and more than a few calls and emails will be made to the utility company, but a small percentage will submit complaints to the ombuds office. Some will make repeated contacts.

All responses can adhere to the BIFF structure, especially to blaming, hostile, threatening complaints. Sometimes an ombuds is dealing with a reasonable complaint about a policy or procedure of an organization that can be resolved fairly easily with sufficient information. Other times, there may be a reasonable complaint against a person within an organization who has acted inappropriately or may be an HCP. Other times, the complainant may be an HCP and the organization acted appropriately. Often the ombuds will not know. BIFF communications work in all of these situations.

## Disability Dispute Example

From: Mrs. Tonia Hilkins
To: Office of the Regional Disability Ombuds

This is the third time I've submitted a complaint to you (and to the DSAB) and I'm hoping to get somewhere this time. I know what is BEST for my disabled son (see my previous emails) and he is not being properly served nor is he being treated with respect…and neither am I!!! The disability agency knows that he needs housing that we cannot afford and they have denied our repeated requests to assist him financially. They claim we shouldn't have made an offer on the house before they approved it…

but we had to get that house before someone else did! It was the perfect house to accommodate my disabled son's wheelchair. They haven't helped us at all. What is THEIR job? Now I come to you and don't get the respect of a response. What is YOUR job? Aren't you supposed to serve the public? We will do whatever is in our power to expose and humiliate the agency and your stupid Ombuds office as well!!!! You should be ashamed of yourselves. I have attached a list of all of the improper actions and inactions that you have taken in regard to our family and my son. I guess I shouldn't be surprised. It's what I've come to expect of everyone who works in government.

## Response #1

Mrs. Hilkins:

We have reviewed your request, including all documents provided by you and by the DSAB regarding your claim. After a thorough review, your claim has been rejected. The DSAB adhered to the applicable regulations and can offer no further options or assistance in the matter. Due to this, we have closed this claim. Please be advised that additional claims cannot be filed for a period of six months from the date of your first claim.

Sincerely,
Helen Gaborsky
Regional Manager

## BIFF CHECKER

**Is a response necessary?**          **YES**

Ombuds must respond. Even without the requirement, a good BIFF response can be helpful.

| Brief? *(2-5 sentences)* | YES |
|---|---|
| At 5 sentences, it's brief. | |

| Informative? *(who, what, when, where, what for)* | YES |
|---|---|
| It is informative, but using a word like "rejected" may feel dismissive and hopeless. | |

| Friendly? | NO |
|---|---|
| It's very stiff and formal. The recipient will likely feel dissed and un-heard. | |

| Firm? | YES |
|---|---|
| Extremely. | |

| Advice? | NO |
|---|---|

| Admonishments? | NO |
|---|---|

| Apologies? | NO |
|---|---|

| **IS IT A BIFF?** | **NO** |
|---|---|

**Response #2**

> Mrs. Hilkins:
>
> We received your email. I'm sorry but there's nothing we can do.
>
> Helen Gaborsky
> Regional Manager

## BIFF CHECKER

Not necessary to even check. It's not even close to being useful. Mrs. Hilkins wants attention and respect. This email response is the exact opposite and it will backfire and elicit more emails from her. This is not a BIFF.

**Response #3**

Dear Mrs. Hilkins:

Thank you for writing. You've spent considerable time trying to resolve this issue, which has likely been quite frustrating for you. I reviewed all documents in your file and contacted DSAB asking them to scour their policies to see if anything could be done. Unfortunately, they cannot find another way to resolve the issue due to statutory requirements; however, they provided information about two organizations that may be able to help (listed below). Please feel free to contact them to explore your options. I along with all involved truly hope you will find a satisfactory solution for you and your son.

Best wishes,
Helen Gaborsky
The Office of the Ombuds

## BIFF CHECKER

| Is a response necessary? | YES |
|---|---|

| Brief? *(2-5 sentences)* | YES |
|---|---|

It may seem somewhat long, but it's not too long for such an important issue. This response may give Mrs. Hilkins confidence that full attention was given to her concern, even if nothing changed.

| Informative? *(who, what, when, where, what for)* | YES |
|---|---|

It is logical and avoids judgment and opinons.

| Friendly? | YES |
|---|---|

Using "Dear" shows respect and friendliness. It has a friendly tone without being overly friendly. Starting with a thank you and ending with "Best wishes" is helpful. Mentioning her son lends a friendly touch.

| Firm? | YES |
|---|---|
| It is matter-of-fact with the pertinent details. | |

| Advice? | NO |
|---|---|
| Is the referral to other resources considered advice? In this case, it's not. It's merely passing along information provided by the organization under fire. | |

| Admonishments? | NO |
|---|---|

| Apologies? | NO |
|---|---|

| IS IT A BIFF? | YES |
|---|---|

**Further Analysis**

This complainant has a very real problem, even if she didn't follow proper procedures. Knowing that she and her son have no recourse puts them in a vulnerable position, which translates to an unsafe position. Fear has taken over. Will the response increase her fear or decrease it? It may increase it, but it was the best BIFF possible under the circumstances. By offering referrals to more appropriate agencies, it is a helpful response even if the essence is a "no." By being friendly, this BIFF response could make all the difference between encouraging or stopping Mrs. Hilkins' angry submissions.

The response needed a little compassion and empathy. Most BIFF responses are meant to set limits on back-and-forth emails when an HCP is involved. However, Mrs. Hilkins needs some empathy to help calm her fear. She's been met with a "no" answer twice already (remember, this was her third submission). Although it's not the ombuds' mandate to solve her problem, a well-crafted BIFF can ease her fears, point her in the right direction and avoid additional complaints. However, some people make it a habit to write regularly to the ombuds.

Just continue writing BIFF responses unless and until policy allows for reduction or stopping responses.

## County Road Dispute Example

To Whom It May Concern:

My 86-year-old parents, who have lived in the same place since 1955 and have paid hundreds of thousands or even millions in all kinds of taxes throughout their lifetime, are being treated horribly. It's keeping me awake at night and I truly can't stop thinking about it. They live a mile off the paved highway, and have to take a gravel road that last mile to their house. Every year the county road department sends the motor graders out to work on all county roads, but on this particular road, they have narrowed it a little bit more each year, making it is almost impossible for two cars to pass each other without going in the ditch, which has very steep banks. I fear they will roll their car. After many complaints to the department, I've had it! I'm done! Someone needs to pay! My parents are very important people in our community and should be treated with respect, especially at 86 years! Obviously, the county wants my parents to die. The governor's office punted on this one and referred me to your office. What are you going to do about it? I want you to demand that the county road department widen the road. I've read the laws and know this is illegal!

Sincerely,
Edith Walker

**Response #1:**

Dear Ms. Walker:

The county road department usually does a good job. I will contact them and see if I can understand why they cannot widen the road. In the meantime, I appreciate your patience.

Sincerely,
Chris Wright, County Ombuds

## BIFF CHECKER

**Is a response necessary?**     **YES**
Because it's his job.

**Brief?** *(2-5 sentences)*     **YES**
Perhaps too brief. It feels abrupt.

**Informative?** *(who, what, when, where, what for)*   **MAYBE**
It says that the ombuds is going to investigate it. However, it already seems to be a one-sided search for information, for "why they cannot widen the road." The ombuds seems to be agreeing with the county road department from the start, when he/she should be totally neutral about where the problem may be.

**Friendly?**     **MAYBE**
Maybe. But again, it seems one-sided against the citizen.

**Firm?**     **MAYBE**
It may pause the angry conversation for now, but because it seems one-sided, the citizen may respond in anger right away or it may become more heated after the ombuds gets more information.

**Advice?**     **NO**

**Admonishments?**     **MAYBE**
"I appreciate your patience" may feel like a manipulation, like "You better be patient."

**Apologies?**     **NO**

## IS IT A BIFF?     **NO**

Let's see if this is better:

**Response #2:**

Dear Ms. Walker:

Thank you for bringing this issue to our attention. I will contact the County Road Department to see what is happening and then get back to you about what we can do. Sometimes it is something that is easily remedied and other times there are policies that limit what they can do. I look forward to helping you address and resolve this issue.

Best wishes,
Chris Wright, County Ombuds

## BIFF CHECKER

| | |
|---|---|
| **Is a response necessary?** | **YES** |
| It's typically not optional for ombuds. | |

| | |
|---|---|
| **Brief?** *(2-5 sentences)* | **YES** |

**Informative?** *(who, what, when, where, what for)*   **YES**
It says that the ombuds will gather information, in a neutral way that is appropriate to the situation. Chris further explains that he/she will see "what we can do," indicating the goal of an action outcome. Lastly, Chris explains two possible outcomes, including that the department may be constrained by policies (so it doesn't feel personal and prepares the citizen for a possible "No" outcome).

**Friendly?**   **YES**
Chris thanks the citizen, explains that Chris will see "what we can do" and "I look forward..." to addressing and resolving the issue.

**Firm?**   **YES**
It certainly ends the hostile communication for now, with action being taken and kind words showing empathy for the citizen.

| Advice? | NO |
|---|---|
| Admonishments? | NO |
| Apologies? | NO |
| **IS IT A BIFF?** | **YES** |

## Conclusion

Whether you represent a company, such as a customer service rep, or whether you are in a neutral role, such as an ombuds, much of your work is done by a written response. A BIFF response can keep it simple and brief, while respecting those who are complaining to you. A BIFF can also help you empathize with a complainant without losing your neutrality.

Just as the customer service rep in the prior chapter should not take a position on whether the airline has done something wrong without a full investigation, an ombuds should not take a position on whether the road department is blameless. Especially when you are dealing with an HCP, you cannot make any assumptions for or against what they are saying. They could be totally accurate about a problem or totally distorting the situation—and have a high conflict personality.

Of course, there are many people who do not have high conflict personalities and have legitimate complaints, who may communicate in writing in an extreme manner when they are upset. In all of these situations, a BIFF communication can calm the situation while reasonably addressing the situation in a fair and efficient manner. Whether or not someone is an ombuds, they can use these principles in analyzing their BIFF communications.

## CHAPTER 6

# BIFFs for Clients

Many people work directly with individual clients these days. Whether you are a professional, a contractor, an artist, a personal assistant, or otherwise, you may find yourself in a tight spot when you have a client who seems intent on ruining your day with yet another demanding email. The pang in your gut when you see that name pop up in your inbox, again. The internal struggle to stop yourself from blasting back with all the pent-up frustration that you've previously held back. Can you feel it?

Most of the time we are able to control our interactions with clients because most don't require BIFF responses, but there are clients who require more attention and delicate handling. Early in our careers we may have made a few mistakes but learned from them (maybe with a hard lesson). It's a good idea to learn to BIFF early on.

But what about the long-term client who you've always felt uneasy about and delicately tiptoed around? Just the thought of receiving an email or call from them fills you with dread. The day comes when you're in a rush or dealing with another client, when the dreaded email from the dreaded client arrives demanding your immediate time and attention. Pronto! Stat! Your fingers fly across the keyboard with all the frustration within, hit send, and immediately regret it.

Anxiety creeps in at the thought of a complaint against your license, or a lawsuit. Maybe neither will happen but the threat looms overhead anyway.

Or it may be the case that you're just in a hurry and don't recognize the hostile email for what it is, possibly because it is nuanced or skimming it doesn't reveal its full punch. So a quick, innocent response is sent, resulting in yet another email but much more hostile, blaming, insulting and demanding.

Whether written out of frustration or expediency, you've increased your own exposure and risk—to your license, financially or otherwise. Awareness is key to prevention. If you have a high conflict client, set up a separate email account to receive those emails, or have them sent to an assistant to review first. Anything that will help you remain aware and alert to the fact that BIFF is required.

If you know you are having a rough day or a busy day, avoid reading email from a high conflict client (unless you know something will truly require immediate action). And most importantly, set limits in advance for all clients, especially the high conflict types, on how they can contact you, when they can expect a response ("I check email once/day and respond within 1 business day"), and other limits that will give you time to think before responding.

## Financial Manager Example

From Carlo to Simon

What the f*** were you thinking? Have you lost your damn mind you MF'ing moron! I told you that was a horrible investment strategy and you didn't listen! Your little "just trust me, I know what I'm doing" speech was tripe. Now I'm faced with taking the loss, putting my entire estate at risk. My only option is to sue you. I told you repeatedly not to put my money in that stock but you didn't listen and that makes you responsible for the loss for NOT doing what your client asked. You're such a loser, man! You're fired! I'm moving my account far from you and the joke of a "firm" you're working for.

Carlo

To the outside observer, it's easy to see blamespeak all over this email. There's intense blame, name-calling, all-or-nothing thinking, unmanaged emotions, threats, etc. If you get a kicked-in-the-gut feeling, make sure to slow down before responding. Let's see if Simon takes that approach:

**Response #1**

Wow! Have you got it backwards! Don't you remember that I told you the decision was up to you. I gave you 3 choices, and you chose this investment. Remember the conversation we had about it? I told you that this was the highest risk, but you insisted that you wanted this approach because it also had the highest potential return on investment. I actually encouraged you to take the lowest risk strategy, given your circumstances. Remember I said that the XYZ plan was probably best for you. Don't you remember!!

## BIFF CHECKER

| | |
|---|---|
| **Is a response necessary?** | **YES** |

Carlo is his client. All professionals have an obligation to communicate with existing clients. But apparently Simon didn't wait a moment to think about his response. He just reacted, as you can see.

| | |
|---|---|
| **Brief?** *(2-5 sentences)* | **MAYBE** |

It gets repetitive.

| | |
|---|---|
| **Informative?** *(who, what, when, where, what for)* | **NO** |

It's totally defensive, emotional, blaming back. While it does attempt to provide some information about Simon giving Carlo choices, it doesn't really provide the information.

| | |
|---|---|
| **Friendly?** | **NO** |

| | |
|---|---|
| Firm? | NO |

By blaming Carlo for his own decisions, he is inviting a defensive response from Carlo, which will probably include a new attack.

| | |
|---|---|
| Advice? | NO |

| | |
|---|---|
| Admonishments? | YES |

"Don't you remember?" Simon is admonishing Carl for not remembering.

| | |
|---|---|
| Apologies? | NO |

| | |
|---|---|
| **IS IT A BIFF?** | **NO** |

Let's see if this is better:

**Response #2**

> Dear Carlo,
>
> I value you as a client and I can understand how upsetting that was for you. We were all really disappointed in what happened with that stock. You may recall that I told you it was the highest risk and recommended a different stock. I have attached my email of January to that effect. However, if you are interested, I can meet with you again and go over some more cautious investments. On the other hand, if you want to go to another firm, it's always up to you. I can easily transfer your account to a new account manager of your choice. Let me know what you decide.
>
> Best regards,
> Simon

## BIFF CHECKER

| | |
|---|---|
| Is a response necessary? | YES |

Carlo is an existing client.

**Brief?** *(2-5 sentences)*                                 **YES**

The length appears appropriate for what needed to be said, since terminating their relationship also needed to be addressed.

**Informative?** *(who, what, when, where, what for)*     **YES**

Simon's email was very straightforward, with the information contained in the prior email attached. It's not at all emotional or defensive.

**Friendly?**                                                **YES**

Simon empathizes with Carlo feeling upset and shares that he and others were also very disappointed. He emphasizes that decisions are up to the client.

**Firm?**                                                    **YES**

He ends the hostile conversation with a choice for his client. There are no emotional hooks for Carlo to keep debating blame.

**Advice?**                                                  **NO**

**Admonishments?**                                           **NO**

**Apologies?**                                               **NO**

## IS IT A BIFF?                                             **YES**

### Put Important Advice and Decisions in Writing

Notice that Simon had previously written an email emphasizing his advice and what choices Carl had. This is essential for those working with clients on important matters: when they are given advice and when they agree on what work needs to be done. You need to take the initiative to do that these days, since there is always the risk of a high conflict client. Of course, you can use the BIFF format for this too. Just keep it brief, informative, friendly and firm.

## Lawyer and Client Example

Ms. Constance Kapar, Attorney at Law:

Thank you for taking time to read my letter. I know you've said that the case is over and there's nothing else you can do to help me, but I can't stop thinking about it, especially the major mistake made in negotiations. We never should have conceded on giving the neighbors healthcare power of attorney over my Uncle Ben. When they approved the surgery which caused his death, I truly believe they killed him. They should not have pressured him. He was so old and trusting. I can't stop wondering why you, as an attorney who specializes in elder law, allowed this to happen; why you advised me to accept their proposal.

The more I think about it, I've truly begun to wonder if there was something going on behind the scenes. I know you and my uncle and the neighbors live in the same small town, so it makes sense that you know each other. Some online searching shows that you attend the same church, so now I'm really suspicious and feeling like the $25k I paid in legal fees, only to end up losing my uncle, was a complete waste. You must have known all along that you were going to persuade me to let them have the healthcare power of attorney.

I'm at a complete loss. I would like my money back. If you don't agree, I've decided to explore my options with another attorney, with the state bar complaints area, and even with law enforcement. Please send the refund to me at this address.

Sincerely,
Serena McCrory

## Response #1

Dear Mrs. McCrory,

We were all deeply saddened by the passing of your Uncle Ben. But at his age and in his condition, surgery always carries a risk to it. Please understand that if he didn't get the surgery, there was also a risk of death. I'm attaching a copy of the letter from his doctor, who said it was about a 50-50 chance of him dying with or without the surgery. I don't remember if you ever saw this letter before, but he sent it to the neighbors before they approved the surgery.

I am disturbed that you imply in your letter that I somehow conspired with his neighbors to swing the healthcare power of attorney over to them. I did no such thing! I am, and have always been, a highly ethical lawyer and I will challenge any attempts you make to tarnish my reputation. You are right that this is a small town, but I have an ethical duty to represent you, my client, without any conflict of interest. I believe I properly represented you and you will not be receiving any refund. I worked tirelessly on your case and any implication that I benefitted financially from your wealthy uncle's death is patently absurd.

Constance Kapar
Attorney at Law

## BIFF CHECKER

| | |
|---|---|
| **Is a response necessary?**<br>Mrs. McCrory is an existing client. | **YES** |
| **Brief?** *(2-5 sentences)*<br>See rest of this analysis. | **NO** |
| **Informative?** *(who, what, when, where, what for)* | **YES and NO** |

At first, it focused on the reality of the risks and a helpful letter is attached. But then it becomes very emotional and defensive. It even suggests that Ms. Kapar benefitted financially from Uncle Ben's death, which Mrs. McCrory never brought up or suggested. This raises a very concerning new question in the reader's mind: Did Ms. Kapar benefit?

| Friendly? | YES and NO |
|---|---|

The first paragraph is friendly, but the second paragraph erases that with its defensiveness.

| Firm? | NO |
|---|---|

The defensiveness is less likely to intimidate Mrs. McCrory and more likely to inspire her to investigate. The idea that the lawyer may have benefitted financially is now a new reason to look deeper.

| Advice? | NO |
|---|---|

| Admonishments? | YES |
|---|---|

This statement definitely feels like an admonishment: "I will challenge any attempts you make to tarnish my reputation."

| Apologies? | NO |
|---|---|

## IS IT A BIFF? NO

**Response #2**

Dear Mrs. McCrory,

We were all deeply saddened by the passing of your Uncle Ben. But at his age and in his condition, surgery always carries a risk to it. Please understand that if he didn't get the surgery, there was also a risk of death. I'm attaching a copy of the letter from his doctor, who said it was about a 50-50 chance of him dying with or without the surgery. I don't remember if you ever saw this letter before, but he sent it to the neighbors before they approved the surgery.

I hope this helps give you some peace that neither you nor I nor the neighbors did anything improper.

Very truly yours,
Constance Kapar
Attorney at Law

## BIFF CHECKER

| | |
|---|---|
| **Is a response necessary?** | YES |
| Mrs. McCrory is an existing client. | |

| | |
|---|---|
| **Brief?** *(2-5 sentences)* | YES |
| Just six sentences. | |

| | |
|---|---|
| **Informative?** *(who, what, when, where, what for)* | YES |
| It focused on the reality of the risks and a helpful letter is attached, and that's it. | |

| | |
|---|---|
| **Friendly?** | YES |
| The first paragraph shows some empathy and the last sentence seeks to give her peace of mind. | |

| | |
|---|---|
| **Firm?** | YES |
| It doesn't put out any negative hooks. However, it also doesn't address the refund issue but the rest of the letter strongly implies the answer by saying that no one did anything wrong. (See discussion below about refunds.) | |

| | |
|---|---|
| **Advice?** | NO |

| | |
|---|---|
| **Admonishments?** | NO |

| | |
|---|---|
| **Apologies?** | NO |

## IS IT A BIFF?　　　　　　　　　　YES

### Don't Suggest the Negative

This letter gives a good example of "suggesting the negative." When communicating with high conflict people or anyone who is upset, you are encouraged to avoiding communicating negative terms. The obvious one above is in Response #1 about *not* benefitting financially. By raising this issue, it suggests that there is something like that going on. If Mrs. McCrory is a little paranoid, she will latch onto that statement and increase her drive to investigate.

But other more common terms are used that should be avoided, like: "conspired with the neighbors" and "tarnish my reputation." This reinforces problem areas and HCPs are very suggestible. Emphasizing that you are *not* giving a refund (see below) will only irritate or further anger the client. Focus on the positive and what really needs to be addressed.

### Addressing Refunds

High conflict people often ask their professionals and other contractors for refunds, because they feel that they have been "done wrong" on a regular basis. If you become a *target of blame* in their minds, then they will feel righteously indignant and demand *all* their money back (because of their all-or-nothing thinking), even if you did nothing wrong. Be prepared for this.

However, there are circumstances where a professional has made a mistake and agrees that they owe a refund. In such cases, it may make a lot of sense to simply give the refund with a brief explanation of what it's for (e.g.: "for the letter with the serious typo that needed correcting"), without apologetic or defensive overtones (which tend to draw an HCPs attention).

## Counselor and Client Example

### From Client to Counselor

After our counseling session yesterday, I realized that I

am falling in love with you. I'm overwhelmed with joy that you seem to care about me so much. You are so understanding of everything I'm going through with my Ex. I'm wondering if you are having the same feelings about me. Can you let me know? I can't wait until next week to see you again.

## From Counselor to Client
### Response #1

I'm sorry, but the ethical rules say that I cannot have a relationship beyond that of a counselor and client with you. If these feelings persist, I will not be able to work with you. I will see you next week as scheduled.

## BIFF CHECKER

**Is a response necessary?**                    YES
This is an existing client.

**Brief?** *(2-5 sentences)*                    YES
But it seems too brief, such as to be abrupt.

**Informative?** *(who, what, when, where, what for)*    **YES and NO**
While it is informative about the ethical rules, it seems defensive and rude. The emotional message is insensitive given the sensitive nature of the client's sharing their feelings.

**Friendly?**                    NO
It seems purposely unfriendly. The counselor is probably frightened by the client's feelings and trying to put up a boundary. There are better ways to communicate about this. (See Response #2 and Professional and Client Relationships below.)

**Firm?**                    NO
Firm does not mean harsh; it means to end a hostile conversation or clear up misinformation. Given the nature of the client's email, this

feels harsh and rejecting. This may trigger a strong reaction in the client that will make things worse and escalate the situation.

| | |
|---|---|
| **Advice?** | **NO** |

| | |
|---|---|
| **Admonishments?** | **YES** |

This statement feels like an admonishment: "If these feelings persist, I will not be able to work with you."

| | |
|---|---|
| **Apologies?** | **NO** |

| | |
|---|---|
| **IS IT A BIFF?** | **NO** |

**Response #2**

Thank you for sharing your feelings with me. Feelings of love sometimes happen in counseling because it is such a personal and emotional relationship. This is something that we should talk about in a live session. While I have warm feelings for you, the goal in counseling is to help you have these kinds of feelings with people in your life who are available for a full relationship. I think I can help you with that. If you think you need to talk about this sooner than next week, let me know and I'll see what I can schedule this week. In the meantime, you may want to write in your journal about this. These feelings may be an important sign of progress in your life. Take care.

## BIFF CHECKER

| | |
|---|---|
| **Is a response necessary?** | **YES** |

This is an existing client with intense emotions which need a response.

| | |
|---|---|
| **Brief?** *(2-5 sentences)* | **YES** |

It's a little long, but fits the situation.

**Informative?** *(who, what, when, where, what for)*   **YES**
The counselor has said they have warm feelings for the client and that the counselor can help have a good relationship with someone who is more available. They should talk in person and can set up an earlier appointment if desired.

**Friendly?**                                    **YES**
The counselor respects the client's feelings and says they have warm feelings for the client.

**Firm?**                                        **YES**
The counselor gently makes clear that this should be discussed in person and offers to schedule an earlier appointment. The counselor also implies that he/she cannot have a love relationship with a client but will help have one with someone who is "available" for a full relationship.

**Advice?**                                      **NO**

**Admonishments?**                               **NO**

**Apologies?**                                   **NO**

**IS IT A BIFF?**                                **YES**
This could be a good BIFF response, but a slightly different one might be needed depending on the client.

**Professional and Client Relationships**
This is almost the opposite situation of what we have been talking about, with angry clients sending hostile messages. In this case, it is about the intense *positive* feelings that can develop in any one-to-one work relationship, especially one in which intense emotions are discussed. For example, it is common for people going through a divorce to fall in love with their therapist or their lawyer, because it is all about intense emotions.

In such situations, there are strict ethical rules about keeping the relationship professional, as those who violate those rules can lose their license to practice therapy, law or other profession, or even go to jail. The burden is on the professional.

Yet it helps for professionals to be respectful of those emotions and not to panic, like the counselor in Response #1 seemed to do. That is why in Response #2 the counselor did not talk about the ethical rules in the email, because that can feel unnecessarily rejecting. It's better to discuss that in person, so long as the counselor feels that they are on solid ground about upholding these rules and boundaries.

Such intimacy can develop in any such close work relationship, so that BIFF responses need to be sensitive and respectful as well as brief, informative, friendly and firm.

## Conclusion

In this chapter we have discussed handling difficult communications for anyone who works closely with individual clients. Such relationships can trigger intense negative or intense positive emotions, so that it is important to handle them in a respectful manner that doesn't get you in trouble. BIFF communications can really help in setting boundaries, setting realistic expectations, clearing up misinformation, maintaining positive relationships or ending relationships respectfully.

When high conflict people are involved, it's especially important to not over-react in anger, defensiveness, or creating unrealistic expectations. Keep in mind that people who love you today could hate you tomorrow, so aim for balanced working relationships with everyone.

In this chapter we talked about putting information in writing when important advice is given and decisions are made. This can be done in the BIFF format and may help you when you are blamed later on when perceptions of advice and decisions are distorted by a possible high conflict client.

We also addressed not suggesting the negative in your language in BIFF responses to angry clients. Keep it brief and focused on the positive options in the present as much as possible.

We also addressed the troublesome issue of refunds, which high conflict clients sometimes demand because of their all-or-nothing perceptions. If they have a legitimate complaint, then deal with it, but briefly as needed.

Overall, working with individual clients can create intimacy which is a particularly tricky area for high conflict people. Using BIFF communications can help you stay balanced, serve your clients well, and protect yourself at the same time.

# SECTION 3

# BIFF for Internal Communications

CHAPTER 7

# BIFFs for Co-workers and Toxic Teams

## Individuals

Email between co-workers is possibly the ripest environment for nastiness, spite, anger and accusations. Over the past 15-20 years, we've been saying that high conflict personalities are increasing in today's society, but as we write this book (2021), we are in the midst of an escalation never before seen in high conflict behaviors on a society-wide level. We've just come upon the year anniversary of the worldwide coronavirus Covid-19 pandemic, which saw the workplace undergo a transition like never before. At least not in the lifetime of most currently in the workplace.

People have shifted to working from home, spending more time on screens than in-person. Fear and anxiety from worrying about the effects of the pandemic—finances, death, long-term damage to health, family, loss—abound. With anxiety comes irritability and frustration, often leading to lack of restraint under normal circumstances but open season for those already on the high conflict end of the spectrum (blame, all-or-nothing, unmanaged emotions, extreme behaviors).

However, whether in a worldwide crisis or not, high conflict people (HCPs) struggle in relationships. The workplace is ripe for hostile email because the majority of one's time spent around others during waking hours is with co-workers. Right brain reactivity is likely to be triggered in HCPs more by the mere fact of being forced to communicate with others 40+ hours/week; it's not optional for them as they are highly unaware.

**Teams**

Imagine the destruction and negative disruption an HCP can have on a team. They are known to divide (called *splitting*) groups of people. They are not known as uniters. Getting anything done is much more difficult as team members either engage with the HCP or disengage and develop work-arounds.

First, let's do some BIFFs for individuals and then a few for teams.

## Example between Co-Workers

> Aaron—I emailed you a week ago about the grid project. As of yet, you haven't responded. Scott said you always email him back promptly. You don't give me the same courtesy or respect. I can't get my work done if you never respond. If that's how it's gonna be, then I'll sit on this project and let it rot while you work on personal stuff. By the way, I've cc'd Dave and Scott as it's time that management learns who is really holding this project up.
>
> Kevin

**First, let's explore if this is a high-conflict email.** It seems to have some high-conflict features, including:

- use of the terms "always" and "never", which possibly indicate all-or-nothing thinking
- use of the term "respect," which may be what Kevin craves
- accusations of working on "personal stuff"
- blaming Aaron while cc'ing the managers

Now, let's try some responses.

## Response #1

Kevin,

As everyone knows, I am swamped with projects right now and yours is the least of my worries. I have bigger fish to fry and Dave and Scott know that. I will get back to you as soon as I can.

Aaron

## BIFF CHECKER

| | |
|---|---|
| **Is a response necessary?** | **YES** |
| Kevin and Aaron are both on a project. | |
| **Brief?** *(2-5 sentences)* | **YES** |
| But it's too brief, which means it's a bit abrupt. | |
| **Informative?** *(who, what, when, where, what for)* | **NO** |
| It's totally defensive, emotional, blaming back. | |
| **Friendly?** | **NO** |
| **Firm?** | **NO** |
| By blaming Aaron for being a nuisance, Aaron is likely to reply further or take it to Dave and Scott. It's not settled down at all. | |
| **Advice?** | **NO** |
| **Admonishments?** | **YES** |
| "Yours is the least" important. "I have bigger fish to fry." These feel like admonishments. | |
| **Apologies?** | **NO** |

## IS IT A BIFF?                                     NO

Let's see if this is better:

**Response #2**

Kevin,

I appreciate your need for information from me on the grid project. I'm swamped right now with other projects, but I will try to get back to you within 24 hours. Thanks!

Aaron

## BIFF CHECKER

| | |
|---|---|
| **Is a response necessary?** | YES |
| They both work on the project. | |

| | |
|---|---|
| **Brief?** *(2-5 sentences)* | YES |
| It's short, but fits the situation. | |

| | |
|---|---|
| **Informative?** *(who, what, when, where, what for)* | YES |
| The main information is that he'll try to get back to him within 24 hours. That's most he can tell him now. | |

| | |
|---|---|
| **Friendly?** | YES |
| "I appreciate your need for information from me." And he closed with "Thanks." That's sufficient for this situation. | |

| | |
|---|---|
| **Firm?** | YES |
| He settled the issue, at least for 24 hours. | |

| | |
|---|---|
| **Advice?** | NO |

| | |
|---|---|
| **Admonishments?** | NO |

| | |
|---|---|
| **Apologies?** | NO |

## IS IT A BIFF?                    YES
This would be a good BIFF response for this situation.

# Example of Co-Workers with a Deadline

**Email from Sophie to Carmen:**

> Carmen: Checking in to see if you have updated the spreadsheets with the actual fiscal year data yet? The deadline is getting close.
>
> Sophie

**Response from Carmen to Sophie:**

> I told you I'd get those done! You don't need to ask. I get my work done and I don't need to be reminded over and over.

**Is this a high-conflict response? It is quite defensive and curt.**

**Response #1**

> From Carmen to Sophie:
>
> You don't have to get snippy about it. Just give me a date to expect them and I'll leave you alone.

## BIFF CHECKER

| | |
|---|---|
| **Is a response necessary?** | MAYBE |
| Sophie still needs the information, but Carmen has already said to leave her alone. Maybe waiting a day or two would help? Hard to say. | |
| **Brief?** *(2-5 sentences)* | YES |
| Probably okay length. | |
| **Informative?** *(who, what, when, where, what for)* | MAYBE |
| It mostly just reiterates what she already wanted, but this is more specific with "give me a date." | |
| **Friendly?** | NO |
| It's reactive and defensive. | |

| | |
|---|---|
| **Firm?** | YES |
| It asks for a clear and simple answer. | |
| **Advice?** | NO |
| **Admonishments?** | YES |
| "You don't have to get snippy about it." | |
| **Apologies?** | NO |
| **IS IT A BIFF?** | **NO** |

### Response #2

Carmen: Great! Just give me a date I can expect to receive them. That's all I need. Thanks.

Sophie

## BIFF CHECKER

| | |
|---|---|
| **Is a response necessary?** | YES |
| If she really needs the information and asks for it this way. | |
| **Brief?** *(2-5 sentences)* | YES |
| It's short, but fits the situation. | |
| **Informative?** *(who, what, when, where, what for)* | YES |
| She just needs a date and that's all. | |
| **Friendly?** | YES |
| "Great!" and "Thanks." The rest is neutral tone. | |
| **Firm?** | YES |
| "That's all I need." | |
| **Advice?** | NO |
| **Admonishments?** | NO |

| Apologies? | NO |
|---|---|

**IS IT A BIFF?**                 **YES**

This would be a good BIFF response for this situation

## Email between Co-Workers about Friendship

Amelia,

This issue between us seems to be never-ending. I've tried being nice, being quiet, being talkative, leaving you alone, and countless other ways to re-establish a good relationship with you…. but nothing works. We were such good friends in the beginning and worked in tandem so well…and then everything changed. You just became so distant and then you became mean and rude. You can't imagine how devastating it is to see the look on your face during meetings. You smile at everyone else but not at me; instead, your face looks cross when you look at me. You treat me differently. Honestly, I simply feel abandoned and left with no choice but to go to Lucy to see if she can fix this thing between us. I don't have much confidence in her ability to fix it—she seems to favor you. If she can't (or won't) help, then I'll go to HR. We just can't go on like this any longer.

Jennifer

**Is this a blamespeak email?** We sometimes expect a hostile email to have loads of exclamation marks, words in ALL CAPS, and accusations, but in some, it's more nuanced. This email is full of blamespeak in that it:

- focuses on a friendship in the workplace, instead of work
- use of the terms "never-ending", "abandoned", "no choice", which are all-or-nothing

- referencing facial expressions and different treatment
- using the manager and HR as a threat to fix her *relationship* issues

**Response #1**

Jennifer

You need to get a life. I mean, really! You need to stop clinging to me and focus on work. That's what happened between us and can't be fixed. You want an intense friendship and I just want to do my job. There's no need to bring Lucy or HR into this. That's just stupid. I'm sick of dealing with you. Leave me alone! We can work together, but we're not going to "friends!" It's not appropriate for the workplace.

Amelia

## BIFF CHECKER

**Is a response necessary?**       **MAYBE**
Maybe. Since Jennifer is so upset, the situation should get a response to calm things down. (Although this won't do it.)

---

**Brief?** *(2-5 sentences)*       **YES**
Probably okay length.

---

**Informative?** *(who, what, when, where, what for)*       **MAYBE**
It makes clear that Amelia doesn't want a friendship and wants to be left alone. Since it's about a friendship and not a necessary work relationship, there's no practical information to exchange.

---

**Friendly?**       **NO**
It's reactive and defensive.

---

**Firm?**       **YES**
It asks to end the communication. But doing it this way probably will

elicit a response from Jennifer, as she will probably feel insulted and possibly abandoned.

| Advice? | NO |
|---|---|

| Admonishments? | YES |
|---|---|

"You need to stop clinging to me."

| Apologies? | NO |
|---|---|

## IS IT A BIFF?                                    NO

**Response #2**

Jennifer

I got your email and I get it that you want a close friendship. While I also enjoyed our early times together, I don't think it's realistic to have such a close relationship with those I work with. I don't mean to seem to favor other people on our team; I'm just trying to get along with everyone. If it seems like I'm being rude, that's not my intent. But I don't want to mislead you into thinking we can be super close. It's best if we keep it as respectful co-workers. If you agree, I can be more relaxed around you. Let's agree to be pleasant co-workers and leave it at that. Ok? You don't have to respond. I'll see you around.

Amelia

## BIFF CHECKER

| Is a response necessary? | MAYBE |
|---|---|

When in doubt, respond with a BIFF response.

| Brief? *(2-5 sentences)* | YES |
|---|---|

This might seem a little long, but it's about setting limits on a friendship, which sometimes takes saying a little more.

**Informative?** *(who, what, when, where, what for)*     **YES**
    It says where she's at in terms of not wanting a close relationship, but a cordial co-worker relationship.

| | |
|---|---|
| **Friendly?** | **YES** |

It's much more respectful while still setting limits.

| | |
|---|---|
| **Firm?** | **YES** |

It tries to settle the issue. Asking "Ok?" is probably not a good idea, but it does add a friendly touch.

| | |
|---|---|
| **Advice?** | **NO** |

| | |
|---|---|
| **Admonishments?** | **NO** |

| | |
|---|---|
| **Apologies?** | **NO** |

| | |
|---|---|
| **IS IT A BIFF?** | **YES** |

### Friendships at Work

This example highlights the problem of getting too close with people at work. High conflict people often are looking for intense friendships at work, because all of their outside relationships have failed. It's best to avoid getting too close to anyone at work, because it's hard to then back off from a close relationship. Some high conflict people become extremely jealous and hostile when someone backs away from them. Better to go slow or keep distance from the start.

## Team Email between Team Members

Team,

I don't like having to do this but you've forced me into bringing it up. You've consistently withheld extremely important information from me when you knew I needed to get my part done. Is it because I identify as nonbinary? Do I not fit YOUR "norm"? It's not fair and I've had it! I'm done!

Jax

**Is this blamespeak?** Yes, and here's why:

- use of the term "forced"
- accusations of withholding information without giving specifics
- accusations of gender inequity, a hot topic that is sure to inflame
- ending with an all-or-nothing position and exclamation
- seems like a rant with no problem-solving of solution focus

**Response #1**

Hi Jax,

I'm not sure what information you're looking for. Can you be more specific, then I'll see if we can provide it.

Take care,

Mary
Santa Fe Team

## BIFF CHECKER

| | |
|---|---|
| **Is a response necessary?** | **YES** |
| Keeping a team on an even keel is important. | |
| **Brief?** *(2-5 sentences)* | **YES** |
| But perhaps too brief. | |
| **Informative?** *(who, what, when, where, what for)* | **YES** |
| It says she's open to providing the information that Jax is asking for. | |

| Friendly? | YES |
|---|---|

She says she'll try to fulfill Jax request.

| Firm? | YES |
|---|---|

It's very straightforward in trying to settle the issue by finding the information that is being sought..

| Advice? | NO |
|---|---|

| Admonishments? | NO |
|---|---|

| Apologies? | NO |
|---|---|

## IS IT A BIFF?                     SOMEWHAT

This would be an okay BIFF response. But could it be better, given the allegations of discrimination?

**Response #2**

Hi Jax,

I'm not sure what information you're looking for. Can you be more specific, then I'll see if we can provide it.

You have also raised a serious concern. Let me know if you would like to meet with me or another team member to discuss it.

Take care,

Mary
Santa Fe Team

## BIFF CHECKER

| Is a response necessary? | YES |
|---|---|

Keeping a team on an even keel is important..

| Brief? *(2-5 sentences)* | YES |
|---|---|

This may be a better approach, so that the allegation of discrimination doesn't go unaddressed.

**Informative?** *(who, what, when, where, what for)*     **YES**
It says she's open to providing the information that Jax is asking for and meeting about the allegation of discrimination.

---

**Friendly?**                                              **YES**
She says she'll try to fulfill Jax request and meet with Jax, if Jax wants.

---

**Firm?**                                                  **YES**
It's straightforward in trying to find the information that is being sought. Mary is also giving Jax an opening without a requirement to meet.

---

**Advice?**                                                **NO**

---

**Admonishments?**                                         **NO**

---

**Apologies?**                                             **NO**

---

**IS IT A BIFF?**                                          **YES**

## Email from Team Leader to Difficult Team Member

BIFF can be used to initiate a communication with a potentially difficult person. Let's look at this example, then see if it could be improved.

Norah,

We hate that it's come to this but we're left with no choice if we want to get the FCC project in on deadline. Frankly, the problem is because of the conflict between you and some members of the team, which has led to the delays. We are exasperated to the point we don't know what to do, so we've decided there'll be no more tip-toeing around you, so we are assigning your tasks to Jason and Lizzy. Please transfer your materials to them by Friday.

Alicia

## BIFF CHECKER

| Is a response necessary? | MAYBE |
|---|---|
| However, this might be better handled in person. | |

| Brief? *(2-5 sentences)* | YES |
|---|---|
| It's a paragraph, but it says more than it needs to. | |

| Informative? *(who, what, when, where, what for)* | MAYBE |
|---|---|
| It says Norah is being pulled from the team, but it also goes into unnecessary personal criticism. | |

| Friendly? | NO |
|---|---|
| Alicia is criticizing Norah and then saying Norah is pulled from the team. Nothing friendly about it. | |

| Firm? | MAYBE |
|---|---|
| It's starting a conflict that will probably get an angry response from Norah. | |

| Advice? | NO |
|---|---|

| Admonishments? | NO |
|---|---|

| Apologies? | NO |
|---|---|

## IS IT A BIFF?                          NO

Let's try to improve it.

**Communication #2**

Norah,

I'm worried about getting the FCC project in on deadline. I've decided I want Jason and Lizzy to handle the part you've been working on. I know this may be frustrating, but I think it's for the best. Please transfer your materials to them by Friday.

If you have any questions, please let me know.

Thanks,
Alicia

## BIFF CHECKER

**Is a response necessary?** **MAYBE**
It might be better handled in person. However, doing it as a written BIFF communication gives Norah the opportunity to save face and just accept this decision, unless she wants to ask questions and discuss.

**Brief?** *(2-5 sentences)* **YES**
It's a paragraph.

**Informative?** *(who, what, when, where, what for)* **YES**
It says Norah is being pulled from the project, but does not go into unnecessary and vague personal criticism.

**Friendly?** **YES**
Alicia says she understands this may be frustrating and offers to discuss if requested.

**Firm?** **YES**
It does not incite resistance, although it may be frustrating and trigger an angry response.

**Advice?** **NO**

**Admonishments?** **NO**

**Apologies?** **NO**

## IS IT A BIFF? **YES**

### Verbal BIFF Communication

Alicia: Norah, I need to talk to you. Is this a good time?

Norah: What do you want to talk about?

Alicia: I'm worried about meeting the deadline on the FCC project, so I'd like to transfer your tasks to Jason and Lizzy. Can you get your work transferred over to them by Friday? Do you have any questions about that?

Norah: Why? That's crazy!

Alicia: I appreciate that you've been working on this, but things have been slowed down by the conflict between you and some members of the team. This is the quickest solution I can think of. If you want to discuss this with the other team members, we can do that after the deadline. Right now, that is the highest priority. Can you get that transferred by Friday? I need your help with this.

Norah: I guess so.

Alicia: Thanks!

## BIFF CHECKER

**Is a response necessary?**                 **YES**
Even when doing this type of in-person communication, it can be helped by taking the BIFF approach.

**Brief?** *(2-5 sentences)*              **YES**
Alicia kept it focused on what needs to be done now.

**Informative?** *(who, what, when, where, what for)*   **YES**
She said Norah is being pulled from the project, but did not go into unnecessary personal criticism.

**Friendly?**                       **YES**

Alicia says she appreciates that Norah has been working on this and offers to discuss it after the deadline, if requested.

| Firm? | YES |
|---|---|

Alicia is clear in her directions and does not open it up for feedback at this time. Of course, if Norah said she wanted more feedback right away, Alicia could go into it. However, if Norah is a high conflict person, she may get into unmanageable emotions and make matters worse. Alicia can help her stay emotionally contained by not opening up unnecessary issues and instead just focusing on what needs to be done now.

| Advice? | NO |
|---|---|
| Admonishments? | NO |
| Apologies? | NO |

| IS IT A BIFF? | YES |
|---|---|

If Norah challenges Alicia strongly, then this could become a job performance issue.

## Avoiding Unnecessary Confrontations with High Conflict People

It is important to realize that high conflict people have a hard time managing themselves. They do better with structure and an emphasis on what to do now, rather than going into emotions, the past, or trying for insight into their own behavior. If you're going to fire such an employee, then that's a different story. But if you're just trying to manage them and they are sufficiently manageable, then focus on being brief, informative, friendly and firm. If several people on the whole team are toxic, then stronger methods may be needed, such as described in the book *It's All Your Fault at Work: Managing Narcissists and Other High-Conflict People.* (Eddy & DiStefano, 2015)

## Conclusion

In this chapter, we addressed using BIFF communications in difficult co-worker and team situations. BIFF can be used to calm conflicts with co-workers, without going unnecessarily into great detail and responding with anger. BIFF can also be used in team situations, to keep things from escalating into a major conflict or distraction. We also looked at how you can use the BIFF format in a verbal situation. BIFF can help you navigate the daily workplace tensions that can often arise, whether you have a high conflict person on the team or are just dealing with stress and deadlines.

## CHAPTER 8

# BIFFs for Your Boss

E ven though our High Conflict Institute website was devoted to divorce and family law back in the beginning in 2007, today the number one search term for information on our website has consistently been "managing my narcissistic boss."

If you've flipped to this chapter first, it's likely that you are in a desperate spot, thirsty for information to alleviate the dread of dealing with your boss. We've been there. And we've advised workers from east to west, north to south, to use BIFF as a viable option for managing the relationship with a difficult boss.

It makes complete sense for some high conflict people (HCPs) to land management and executive positions or to own and run a business. Some HCPs are naturally driven to feel (be) superior and/or to dominate others. Rising to leadership positions is the most natural path along their trajectory because the need for them to dominate and to be superior isn't optional. It's hard-wired into their psyche and maybe even into their DNA. It is their operating system. You won't beat it by railing against it or arguing with it.

The problem we run into is that we don't understand that the HCP boss is ruled by fear. They live in a constant loop like this: when they feel superior and/or dominating, they feel okay. When those fears are triggered by an outsider (usually unwittingly by the outsider), their reactionary brain does what it takes to get back to the *okay* state again. How do they do this?

By one-upping and dissing. Whatever it takes to make them feel superior and dominating again. This is where we see lots of bullying.

So, stick to a structure, the BIFF structure, when communicating with them. Otherwise, you will get triggered, defensive, defeated, and ultimately you lose. Many people give up because they've lost hope that things will ever change. Dreading your job because of your boss is debilitating.

The good news is there's hope. You can gain ground and feel more satisfied with your job when you take control of the interactions. The first step is using BIFF in all communications. It helps you avoid the landmines that spark their defensiveness and supreme need to put you down, undermine you, devalue you, and make you look bad.

BIFF puts you in control of the interactions.

## Example with Ethical Implications

**Email string between boss and employee:**

> **Boss:** I thought I was clear about updating the numbers in that report for the committee. They don't look changed to me??? Time is short – come on!

> **Response from Employee:** Look. I'm sorry and I know you're stressed. But I can't in good conscience change the numbers. It's really hard for me to say this without stepping on toes, but the numbers aren't valid and there's the risk of us getting found out. Anyone can do a little searching online to discover this. Then we'll all be in hot water. So, I'm trying to help you out here. Maybe you should get a second opinion from legal. That's my advice.

> **Boss:** You are paid to do what you're told, so do it! My Dad started this company—he would have told you the very same thing! Damn, I work with a bunch of idiots that can't do what they're told!

## BIFF CHECKER

| | |
|---|---|
| **Is a response necessary?** | YES |

It's the boss and it's the employee's job.

| | |
|---|---|
| **Brief?** *(2-5 sentences)* | YES |

| | |
|---|---|
| **Informative?** *(who, what, when, where, what for)* | YES |

It explains why the employee is not willing to do the "update."

| | |
|---|---|
| **Friendly?** | YES |

It makes an effort: "I'm trying to help you out here."

| | |
|---|---|
| **Firm?** | YES |

It's clear that the employee is not going to do what the boss wants. The employee is actually trying to pass the buck to legal.

| | |
|---|---|
| **Advice?** | YES |

Passing the issue to legal was the employee's advice.

| | |
|---|---|
| **Admonishments?** | NO |

| | |
|---|---|
| **Apologies?** | YES |

By starting with "I'm sorry," it sounds like an apology. But it's really not, which often irritates a person who momentarily thought it was.

## IS IT A BIFF?     NO

This was not really a BIFF response, but it's not bad. Since it has already been sent, should the employee respond further? Let's see.

**Response #2**

**Employee**: I appreciate your frustration, but I just can't do this for the reasons I already explained. I'm doing my job and looking out for your interests.

## BIFF CHECKER

| | |
|---|---|
| **Is a response necessary?** | YES |

It's the boss and he/she has reiterated their demand for action.

**Brief?** *(2-5 sentences)*         **YES**
> It's just two sentences, which is an appropriate length for a follow-up response on the same subject.

**Informative?** *(who, what, when, where, what for)*   **YES**
> It explains that the employee is staying firm in not doing the "up-date." It is also shorter than the first response, because it doesn't bring up any new issues.

**Friendly?**         **YES**
> "I appreciate your frustration." "I'm looking out for your interests."

**Firm?**         **YES**
> It's really clear that the employee is not going to do what the boss wants. This doesn't bring up any new issues to keep the conflict going.

**Advice?**         **NO**

**Admonishments?**         **NO**

**Apologies?**         **NO**

## IS IT A BIFF?         YES
> This is a good follow-up BIFF response and appropriate to send to or at least reply to the boss and possibly calm the boss, rather than not responding at all.

## Arrogant Boss Example

**From:** Ian
**To:** Ruth

Ruth—I'm not sure how I should handle this, so I've been holding it in for a long time. When you assigned me to the density analysis project, I took it very seriously and spent months doing the research. It was my first time on such a large and significant project. To discover now that you've had someone working on the same project in the background the whole time is massively discouraging and maddening. It feels like my time has been wasted and that you don't have confidence in my abilities. I know this is government work and the budgeted monies "must be spent so we don't lose them in next year's budget", but it seems a waste of taxpayer money. I don't know what my question is—I'm just so frustrated and perplexed. Is there any way you can help me understand this better? Should I have done things differently?

. . . . . . . . .

**From:** Ruth
**To:** Ian

Ian,

Sure I can help you "understand this better." You're new. You don't communicate. You don't participate in meetings. You lack focus. Ultimately, this is your fault. I waited and waited for you to come to me, but you never did. You somehow think I'm supposed to come to you, but apparently you don't possess or were never taught about levels of authority or about respect. Here, I'll spell it out for you...slowly: I am at a "high-er" level of authority. You are at a "low-er" level, with zero authority. I am the boss. You are not. You work for me. I don't work for you. I make the rules. You follow the rules. You report to me. I don't report to you. Getting the picture now?

Don't ever accuse me again of wasting "taxpayer money." You are the one who wasted it (see above)!

Ruth

## Response #1

**From:** Ian
**To:** Ruth

Ruth—I guess I need to apologize to you for not asking for more guidance earlier. I know I'm not the best communicator, but I know that I generally do a good job otherwise. I'm sorry that I disappointed you and will try to do better next time.

But I think you need to take some responsibility too. The way you treat me and others in our department makes people afraid to talk to you and speak up at meetings. Just look at how you have written back to me with nothing but criticism. It makes me feel like quitting this job all together. Please back off and tell me what you want me to know in a friendlier manner in the future.

## BIFF CHECKER

**Is a response necessary?**                           **MAYBE**
The employee, Ian, has just been belittled and, frankly, harassed for asking a legitimate question. If Ian wants to calm the situation without making a big deal of it, a BIFF response might be an easy and balanced way to go.

---

**Brief?** *(2-5 sentences)*                           **MAYBE**
It seems a little long, but not real long.

---

**Informative?** *(who, what, when, where, what for)*   **MAYBE**
It explains that the employee wants more guidance. But it's also defensive by the employee criticizing the boss.

---

**Friendly?**                                          **YES**
It makes an effort: "I'm sorry I disappointed you." But it also criticizes the boss.

**Firm?**                                          **NO**

By criticizing an angry and arrogant boss, the negative feedback will easily trigger an intense backlash.

**Advice?**                                        **YES**

The employee is giving the boss advice on how to manage. This will not go over well.

**Admonishments?**                                 **YES**

The employee admonishes the boss to back off.

**Apologies?**                                     **YES**

It is a true apology, but it will likely be used against the employee in the future. "Remember when you said you were sorry that you weren't a good communicator? Well, you're doing it again! I'm going to tell everyone you admitted it yourself!"

## IS IT A BIFF?                                    **NO**

### Response #2

From: Ian
To: Ruth

Thank you for responding to my request for feedback. I will do my part to request more guidance on projects in the future. Please let me know if you have any specific suggestions for me in the future. I want to do well in your department and I appreciate all the help you wish to offer.

## BIFF CHECKER

**Is a response necessary?**                       **YES**

Ian has been belittled and harassed for asking a legitimate question. A BIFF response may help calm the situation as well as create a paper trail of his efforts to address the harassment directly himself if he ever needs to take it to a higher level above Ruth.

| | |
|---|---|
| **Brief?** *(2-5 sentences)* | **YES** |

| | |
|---|---|
| **Informative?** *(who, what, when, where, what for)* | **YES** |

He says we will try harder to speak up and is open to his boss' suggestions. It has a future focus, rather than defending and justifying the past.

| | |
|---|---|
| **Friendly?** | **YES** |

Ian thanks Ruth and expresses his openness to feedback.

| | |
|---|---|
| **Firm?** | **YES** |

He leaves no hooks to trigger a backlash. Ironically, by inviting Ruth to give him specific feedback, she is in a harder position to complain if she lets it build up and then blasts him like she did above.

| | |
|---|---|
| **Advice?** | **NO** |

By expressing his openness to her feedback, he is asking for advice, not giving it.

| | |
|---|---|
| **Admonishments?** | **NO** |

| | |
|---|---|
| **Apologies?** | **NO** |

He has expressed his future openness to feedback without saying "I'm sorry." This addresses the problem by taking responsibility going forward, not focusing on blame looking backward.

| | |
|---|---|
| **IS IT A BIFF?** | **YES** |

## New Difficult Manager Example

Ken has just been promoted to a Project Manager position in his division. He hears that another team member, Robert, is angry that Ken got the job instead of him.

Robert—

I've just heard that you think I'm not suited for the Project Manager position. Really? What would you know? I can't believe that you said that. After 15 years here, you think I don't know what the job entails. I've been essentially doing that job for the PM's over the years who don't know HOW to do that job?

Also, just to let you know, as the new PM I just gave the go ahead for the new policies to be rolled out this quarter. Before you go mouthing off about that, everyone at my first meeting gave it a big thumbs up. You did not even have the decency to come to the meeting. I know you wanted the PM role. They must have seen something more in me than you. It happens.

Ken

## Response #1

Ken –You are as arrogant as they come. This email you have sent me is a good example. I am going to be forwarding this to upper management and I hope they quickly reconsider their decision to promote you.

Robert

## BIFF CHECKER

| | |
|---|---|
| **Is a response necessary?** | **MAYBE** |

Ken seems to have shown that he may not be qualified for his management position. But this may not be the best way to deal with that.

| | |
|---|---|
| **Brief?** *(2-5 sentences)* | **YES** |

| | |
|---|---|
| **Informative?** *(who, what, when, where, what for)* | **YES** |

Robert explains that he's forwarding the email to upper management, but it clearly is a defensive, angry act and not just straight information.

| | |
|---|---|
| **Friendly?** | **NO** |

Not at all.

| Firm? | NO |
|---|---|
| Robert invites an escalation of conflict. | |

| Advice? | NO |
|---|---|

| Admonishments? | YES |
|---|---|
| Telling Ken that he is arrogant implies an admonishment to cut it out. | |

| Apologies? | NO |
|---|---|

## IS IT A BIFF? NO

**Response #2**

Clearly Ken is writing blamespeak, which is not a good sign in a new manager. But let's suppose that Robert may not be happy, but wants to stay on good terms for the time being and isn't bad-mouthing him to anyone. He might just try to calm the situation with this response.

> Ken –
>
> Congratulations on becoming the new PM. It's too bad because of COVID that we couldn't have a gathering to welcome you to the new position.
>
> Just to let you know, I am not telling others on the team that you are not qualified. I was unable to come to the meeting because of a pre-existing schedule conflict. I look forward to accomplishing our goals this year. If you still feel there is tension between us, I'm open to discussing it at any time.
>
> Best wishes,
> Robert

## BIFF CHECKER

| Is a response necessary? | YES |
|---|---|
| Since Robert wants to calm Ken, a BIFF is a good way to respond to | |

Ken's written anger. This could open the door to a face-to-face meeting, which would be the best way to deal with this.

| | |
|---|---|
| **Brief?** *(2-5 sentences)* | **YES** |
| It's just six sentences. | |

| | |
|---|---|
| **Informative?** *(who, what, when, where, what for)* | **YES** |
| Robert explains that he wishes Ken well, that he's not trying to undermine Ken, and that he's open to discussing any concerns. | |

| | |
|---|---|
| **Friendly?** | **YES** |
| Robert says congratulations and closes with "Best Wishes." | |

| | |
|---|---|
| **Firm?** | **YES** |
| Robert ends the controversy and is open to meeting, if that's what Ken wants. | |

| | |
|---|---|
| **Advice?** | **NO** |

| | |
|---|---|
| **Admonishments?** | **NO** |

| | |
|---|---|
| **Apologies?** | **NO** |

| | |
|---|---|
| **IS IT A BIFF?** | **YES** |

## Conclusion

One of the biggest problems in today's work world is high conflict managers. They use blamespeak a lot with their teams, but upper management may know nothing about it. Employees coping with HCP managers can benefit from writing BIFF communications on a regular basis (initiating discussions as well as responding). This is especially true, because the paper trail at work can come back to bite employees based on their communications with their managers as well as with their co-workers. Keeping the BIFF method posted nearby one's computer can help a lot, especially during those high conflict moments.

## CHAPTER 9

# BIFFs for Employees

Stakes are high in interactions with employees even in the healthiest of work environments. In the past 5-10 years, workers in some countries, particularly in the U.S., have become emboldened and empowered to make demands in a more hostile and aggressive manner than in the past. Ranging from the mildly dissatisfied to the aggressive, employees are increasingly losing restraint and making their demands known.

Cancel culture has taken hold as well. Groups of employees, both large and small, band together to make demands on the organization, on management. In some cases, a group of employees has successfully demanded the firing of a co-worker or manager. Right or wrong, employees in many organizations may have the vocal authority to accomplish such a firing.

Imagine yourself in the position of receiving a letter or email from the employees. How would you respond to the demands if you did not agree with them? Sadly, this is becoming more common. The reality must be acknowledged. Learning *how* to respond must be refined and be better.

Even a small business with one or two employees has to deal with complicated interactions. Often, small business owners have a full plate and limited bandwidth to address employee issues, eventually bubbling into something larger. A distracted and busy owner or manager may not recognize the seriousness of an unhappy employee's email, and respond off the cuff instead of stepping back for a minute to form an appropriate response. The employee's dissatisfaction and hostility may increase proportionately until everyone in the office (and outside in some cases) is miserable.

Whether large or small, profit or non-profit, using BIFF to respond decreases conflict instead of increasing it.

Prioritizing communications with employees is a risk management tool that can help you avoid complaints and lawsuits. It is a time management tool that can save countless hours of worrying about *how* to respond, *whether* to respond and re-writing it countless times.

## Becoming a New Manager Example

In this example, Nina has just been hired from outside as the new manager for a department. Zachary has worked in that department for over five years and also applied for the job—but didn't get it. Nina hears that Zach is telling the other employees that she is not qualified and that he should have gotten the job. The following is an example of attempting a BIFF communication to initiate a conversation, rather than as a response.

**Communication #1**

> Dear Zachary,
>
> I hear rumors that you are trying to undermine me in my new position as Department Manager. This will not be tolerated. You must cease and desist immediately, otherwise I will consider disciplinary action or removal from the department. Am I understood?
>
> Nina

## BIFF CHECKER

Is a response necessary?                    MAYBE
This is an important issue for a new manager to address before things get out of hand. Of course, it might be handled better in person or a face-to-face virtual meeting.

| Brief? *(2-5 sentences)* | YES |
|---|---|

| Informative? *(who, what, when, where, what for)* | MAYBE |
|---|---|

While it does inform that action might be taken, it seems more defensive and hostile than providing any useful information.

| Friendly? | NO |
|---|---|

Not at all.

| Firm? | MAYBE |
|---|---|

It may intimidate Zachary into stopping or it may just inflame him to embark on a more intense challenge to her authority.

| Advice? | NO |
|---|---|

| Admonishments? | YES |
|---|---|

This is clearly an admonishment: "This will not be tolerated."

| Apologies? | NO |
|---|---|

## IS IT A BIFF?  NO

**Communication #2**

Dear Zachary,

As the new manager, I am going to be meeting one-to-one with key team members in the coming weeks. Given how long you have been on the team, I would like to meet with you in the next week. I am interested in your ideas for how we can improve the department and any concerns you may have. I will discuss some of my ideas.

I would like to meet next Thursday at 8:30am or Friday at 10:00am. Let me know your preference by Monday morning. I look forward to a productive year.

Nina

## BIFF CHECKER

| Is a response necessary? | YES |
|---|---|

Nina needs to get a handle on this situation and setting up a meeting is routinely done by email. By meeting one-to-one, Nina can defuse any complaints that Zachary may have while also building a productive relationship. This approach is far better than a stern warning without empathy by email.

| Brief? *(2-5 sentences)* | YES |
|---|---|

It's only six sentences.

| Informative? *(who, what, when, where, what for)* | YES |
|---|---|

She explains what she hopes to address and her openness to his concerns.

| Friendly? | YES |
|---|---|

She implies that he has important knowledge for the department and that she values meeting with him early on.

| Firm? | YES |
|---|---|

Nina has made it clear that a meeting will happen, but she has also said that he can choose one of two dates. During their meeting she can also discuss setting limits on him bad-mouthing her (if this is true) more effectively than doing it by email, such as in Communication #1.

| Advice? | NO |
|---|---|

| Admonishments? | NO |
|---|---|

| Apologies? | NO |
|---|---|

## IS IT A BIFF?         YES

This is a good BIFF communication.

## Example of a Small Business Manager

This is another example of a manager initiating a communication with an employee, whose father owns the business.

**Communication #1:**

> Mindy—I know you don't want to hear this but the time has come. I've overheard how you talk to customers on the phone. You can't use that tone with them and you can't swear at them . . . even if they are late paying their bill. Several are long-term customers who are used to being handled with care. I'm in a tough position as your boss, since your Dad is *my* boss. I've let it slide for several months because of that but eventually he's going to be on my a\*\* and I could lose my job. Come on, just tone it down please.
>
> Rob

Here is the response that Rob anticipates that he would get:

> Hey Rob -
>
> How dare you! F\*#& YOU! My dad wouldn't do anything about it anyway! He doesn't really give a sh\*\* about anything or anyone except this place!
>
> M

Rob wants to re-write it as a BIFF communication before he sends it out, to avoid risking the type of response he imagined above.

### BIFF CHECKER

**Is a response necessary?**                    **MAYBE**
As Mindy's manager, he needs to address this issue. However, it might be better in person.

**Brief?** *(2-5 sentences)*  MAYBE
> It seems to bring in unnecessary issues.

**Informative?** *(who, what, when, where, what for)*  YES
> He is suggesting using a better tone so that they don't offend long-term customers.

**Friendly?**  MAYBE
> He's trying to be friendly by saying that he waited to tell her this, that he understands she won't want to hear it, and that he could get fired. But these don't work to make it friendly and they suggest a negative response from her, which is usually counter-productive.

**Firm?**  NO
> He imagines she will react angrily as it is written now.

**Advice?**  YES
> He's trying to teach her what not to do.

**Admonishments?**  YES
> He's admonishing her to "tone it down."

**Apologies?**  MAYBE
> He says "I know you don't want to hear this."

## IS IT A BIFF?  NO

As written, it would not be a BIFF communication. Here's a second try with a whole different "tone."

**Communication #2**

> **From:** Rob
> **To:** Mindy
>
> Mindy—I hope you are enjoying working at your father's business. I have a suggestion that I believe will give you some good job skills for the future anywhere you work, including here. If someone is late paying their bill, use a friendly tone of voice to inspire them *to help you out.* Let

them know you understand it's a hard time for everyone, but we need to be paid. It's amazing how a kind word and helping you out can inspire people sometimes.

And that way you would help me out too, because you and I and your Dad need to have happy customers to stay in business.

Thanks for keeping this in mind.
Rob

## BIFF CHECKER

**Is a response necessary?**      **YES**
He's the manager and she is an employee in need of guidance. However, there is still the question of whether this would be better done in person.

**Brief?** *(2-5 sentences)*      **YES**
Perhaps a little long, but still only seven sentences.

**Informative?** *(who, what, when, where, what for)*      **YES**
He explains a good customer service approach.

**Friendly?**      **YES**
He hopes she's enjoying her job and thanks her at the end.

**Firm?**      **YES**
He doesn't put out any hooks to trigger an angry response. He leaves it up to her if she wants more suggestions.

**Advice?**      **MAYBE**
He's her manager giving her some suggestions, so it's not like angry advice. It's just part of his job.

**Admonishments?**      **NO**

**Apologies?**      **NO**

## IS IT A BIFF?      YES

## Example of Laying off an Employee

This is another example of a communication that initiates the conversation. Here is the manager's first draft, which hasn't been sent.

**Communication #1**

Mallory,

I'm sorry to do this by email, but the pandemic has us using email primarily, as we now work from home. I'll get right down to it. We've analyzed the budget and roles in the company and will need to make changes if we're to survive, including cutting projects and downsizing. Unfortunately, one of the positions is yours. Again, I hate to do this by email but I thought it might be easier for you to hear it by email rather than by phone, so you would have time to absorb and think about it.

In consideration of finances, if you'd like to work for another month, just say the word.

Neera and I are happy to write a letter of recommendation whenever you need it.

You've been a valuable member of the team and we're sorry it's come to this.

Sincerely,
Angela (and Neera)

Angela imagines that Mallory will respond something like this:

Neera and Angela:

I'll think about your proposal. I'm not overly inclined to work with you another month but I'll consider it.

I may well decide not to work at all going forward, but I'd appreciate a letter of recommendation from Neera. I doubt Angela's would be sincere, so it's not wanted.

Thanks for your email and the timing. It's the kind of thing I've come to expect of you, Angela.

## BIFF CHECKER

**Is a response necessary?**        **YES**

The employee needs to know this information. Angela even says phone might be nicer, but email gives Mallory a chance to think about it and her response.

**Brief?** *(2-5 sentences)*        **MAYBE**

It gets a little repetitive.

**Informative?** *(who, what, when, where, what for)*    **YES**

It explains the lay off and why, as well as giving her options.

**Friendly?**        **YES**

Angela says Mallory is a valuable member of the team and that they'll write a letter of recommendation.

**Firm?**        **YES**

Angela doesn't leave any hooks to trigger Mallory more than the news will itself.

**Advice?**        **NO**

**Admonishments?**        **NO**

**Apologies?**        **YES**

She says she's sorry it's come to this. Ordinarily, that would be a really good thing to say to an ordinary person. But if she anticipates that Mallory is a high conflict person, then it's better to leave it out because it may be interpreted by Mallory as Angela doing something wrong.

## IS IT A BIFF?        NO

## Communication #2

Mallory,

This pandemic continues to be crazy with us still working from home. I hope you're staying safe and warm.

As you know, the pandemic has really impacted our business. We've analyzed the budget and roles in the company and will need to make changes if we're to survive, including cutting projects and downsizing. Unfortunately, one of the positions is yours. I wanted to give you the heads up right away so you can absorb it, then we can talk by phone if you wish.

In consideration of finances, if you'd like to work for another month, just say the word. Neera and I are happy to write a letter of recommendation whenever you need it.

You've been a valuable member of the team and we're truly sad that it's come to this.

Sincerely,
Angela (and Neera)

## BIFF CHECKER

**Is a response necessary?**                    **YES**
The employee needs to know this information. Angela explains that she can talk by phone now that Mallory has the basic news.

**Brief?** *(2-5 sentences)*                    **YES**
It seems to fit the circumstances with a layoff, when a little longer may be more reasonable.

**Informative?** *(who, what, when, where, what for)*    **YES**
It explains the lay off and why, as well as giving her options.

**Friendly?**                    **YES**
Angela says she's a valuable member of the team and that they'll write a letter of recommendation.

| | |
|---|---|
| Firm? | YES |
| Angela does not leave any hooks to trigger Mallory more than the news will itself. | |
| Advice? | NO |
| Admonishments? | NO |
| Apologies? | NO |
| **IS IT A BIFF?** | **YES** |

## Employee Upset with New Duties Example

Lior,

To be perfectly honest, I feel like quitting and I'm mad at you. I see your attitude toward me and my role here. I don't think it's dawned on you how much your attitude has alienated me.

To be clear, I don't want to take on the new duties you've suggested. I'm sure I could learn it eventually; however, I will never be efficient at it and it's not a good decision. You don't hire an eye doctor to do brain surgery. Plus, I would hate every minute of it. I'm good at a lot of other things.

Thanks,
Maggie

**Response #1**

Dear Maggie,

Unfortunately, there's nothing we can do about this. I've looked at all the options. These new duties need to be handled by you. You are the most appropriate person. They are not that different or difficult. It's just an adjustment and we all have to make adjustments.

I don't appreciate your talking down to me with your doctors' example.

Lior

## BIFF CHECKER

| Is a BIFF communication necessary? | YES |
|---|---|
| This is an employee issue that needs to be addressed. | |

| Brief? *(2-5 sentences)* | YES |
|---|---|

| Informative? *(who, what, when, where, what for)* | YES |
|---|---|
| Lior makes it clear that there are no options here. | |

| Friendly? | NO |
|---|---|
| There are no kind words. | |

| Firm? | YES |
|---|---|
| Lior does not leave any specific hooks to respond to, but it does feel harsh. | |

| Advice? | NO |
|---|---|

| Admonishments? | MAYBE |
|---|---|
| Don't talk down to me. | |

| Apologies? | NO. |
|---|---|

## IS IT A BIFF?                NO, close but not quite.

**Response #2**

Dear Maggie,

I appreciate all of the work you have done for our organization. At this point in time, these new duties are needed and you are the most appropriate person to take them on. I realize I may have been abrupt in making these changes without really discussing them in detail first with you.

I'll try not to do that in the future. It is a time of rapid change, so we all need to adjust the best we can.

Hang in there!
Lior

## BIFF CHECKER

| | |
|---|---|
| **Is a response necessary?** | YES |
| This is an important issue raised by the employee. | |

| | |
|---|---|
| **Brief?** *(2-5 sentences)* | YES |

| | |
|---|---|
| **Informative?** *(who, what, when, where, what for)* | YES |
| It focused on necessary duties. | |

| | |
|---|---|
| **Friendly?** | YES |
| Lior thanked Maggie for her contributions and will try to discuss changes in more detail first in the future.. | |

| | |
|---|---|
| **Firm?** | YES |
| No hooks left out to trigger Maggie. | |

| | |
|---|---|
| **Advice?** | NO |

| | |
|---|---|
| **Admonishments?** | NO |

| | |
|---|---|
| **Apologies?** | NO |
| Lior did say that he would try to discuss changes beforehand in more detail with Maggie in the future, which describes a solution for the future rather than an apology for the past. | |

| | |
|---|---|
| **IS IT A BIFF?** | **YES** |

## Enraged Employee Example

I couldn't be any angrier than I am right now! If you were on fire, I wouldn't walk across the street to spit on you!!! How could you embarrass me like that in front

of all the other servers and cooks?!?!?! I was so humiliated and felt so disrespected. I've NEVER bullied anyone—ever! How could you call me a bully? Just because
someone gets their shorts in a knot over getting yelled
at because they're not doing their actual job! I'm not a
bully and NO ONE has EVER called me a BULLY! It
just doesn't even make sense! In fact, everyone else here
thinks of me as a hero and protector! I am SO done with
this place! And with YOU! I should smash your face in!

Todd

### Response #1

Todd – I am just doing my job. Your anger is a problem
and we need to have a meeting about it.

Cecelia

## BIFF CHECKER

**Is a response necessary?**  **YES**
This is a situation of potential violence with threats of bodily harm
and should be taken very seriously. The organization's policies may
have a procedure for dealing with such threats, including who should
deal directly with Todd and whether it is a termination issue or if he
needs to take a few days off. If Cecelia is involved with any disciplinary
measures, she should not deal with him alone.

**Brief?** *(2-5 sentences)*  **YES**
Perhaps appropriately so.

**Informative?** *(who, what, when, where, what for)*  **YES**
Todd needs to meet with somebody.

**Friendly?**  **NO**
It's too brief and abrupt for that. But it would be better if it did have
somewhat of a friendly tone to help calm him.

| Firm? | YES |
|---|---|
| There are no hooks, but it is abrupt. | |

| Advice? | NO |
|---|---|

| Admonishments? | NO |
|---|---|

| Apologies? | NO |
|---|---|
| She says she's sorry it's come to this. Ordinarily, that would be a really good thing to say to an ordinary person. But if she anticipates that Mallory is a high conflict person, then it's better to leave it out because it may be interpreted by Mallory as Angela doing something wrong. | |

## IS IT A BIFF?     **NO, NOT REALLY.**

**Response #2**

> Todd – I appreciate all of your good work here. This is too important for us to try to discuss by email. I will get back to you to arrange a meeting.

> Take care,
> Cecelia

## BIFF CHECKER

| Is a response necessary? | YES |
|---|---|
| Todd is super angry and needs to be calmed down and his behavior responded to. | |

| Brief? *(2-5 sentences)* | YES |
|---|---|

| Informative? *(who, what, when, where, what for)* | YES |
|---|---|
| It says all that needs to be said: we need to have a meeting to address this. | |

| Friendly? | YES |
|---|---|
| It says: "I appreciate your work," and "Take care." | |

| | |
|---|---|
| Firm?<br>It doesn't leave any hooks to feed the conflict. | YES |
| Advice? | NO |
| Admonishments? | NO |
| Apologies? | NO |

## IS IT A BIFF?                                    YES

### Violence and Threats of Violence

This example raises the issue of violence in the workplace. When threats of violence occur, they need to be taken seriously. We know of several situations in which violence was preceded by written threats like this. This little book does not go into what policies and procedures an organization should have, but an essential part of all of those should be communicating in the BIFF format. This can immediately calm a situation, especially if those around an angry employee know to avoid blamespeak in response to the anger. If all responses are BIFF responses when dealing with this employee, there is much less likelihood that he will escalate into actual violence.

### Public Praise and Private Criticism

One of the issues that often comes up with difficult employees is when and where to give them feedback. In this scenario, it sounds like the employee got some public negative feedback from the manager: "How could you embarrass me like that in front of all the other servers and cooks?!?!?! I was so humiliated and felt so disrespected." This often happens when things build up without being addressed early on in private.

The general principle here is "public praise and private criticism." Remembering this can help many managers avoid unnecessary and dramatic employee upsets.

## Conclusion

Upset employees can be one of the biggest sources of stress for managers. These examples provide words that managers can use in dealing with difficult or high conflict employees, as well as dealing with ordinary moments when employees write upsetting emails and texts. In today's work environment there is more risk of blamespeak—because it is pervasive throughout society right now—but there are also more opportunities to communicate effectively in response to it using BIFF communications.

Keep in mind that BIFF is a tool and not a rule. You may choose to write your communications slightly or significantly differently from the ways we have proposed in this chapter. That is up to you. We hope you can integrate these ideas into your individual and/or organizational ways of communicating, especially when employees are upset. In short, BIFF communications can be quick and routine and get to the point, while also calming conflicts.

## CHAPTER 10

# BIFFs for Business Partners, Committees and Board Members

Millions may be at stake or a mere dollar. Most communications that involve blamespeak are not about the issue at hand. As we like to say, "The issue's not the issue" with blamespeak and especially with high conflict people.

Whether the stakes are high or not, caution must be taken to avoid the communication landmines and pitfalls. BIFF saves time. Time is money.

## Board Members & Committees

The more people that are involved in communications, the higher risk that blamespeak will be encountered. Some corporate boards rarely or never experience blamespeak. Many committees, non-profit boards, and other groups that make decisions jointly may also run smoothly. But when blamespeak happens, many are taken by surprise, especially by the intensity of the blamespeak.

Some react immediately without thinking it through. Others suffer silently, wondering if they are the ones who are out of step. The result is often an escalation of emotions and frustration. A blamespeaker may not be able to stop themselves from continuing the blaming cycle, so those interacting and responding to them must stop it. Sometimes a board, committee, or group may even split into factions over those supportive of the blamespeaker and those who see how destructive he or she is. This can be a big problem with people who are not used to group decision-making and may want to play a more disruptive or dictatorial role.

**Business Partners**

In business school we're taught that partnerships are like marriage and have similar failure rates. In marriage, love at first sight isn't usually a good predictor of a lasting marriage. In business, an incredible business idea isn't a good predictor of a lasting partnership.

We have consulted with many business partners who have discovered that one of their partners was a blamespeaker. The blamespeaker may have yelled a lot at their staff, or blamed other partners when speaking to the public or important colleagues, or directly attacked their partner(s) verbally and in writing on a regular basis. Reasonable partners are looking for tools to manage, improve or end their relationships with partners who are blamespeakers.

As the authors of this book, we have lots of tools and ideas to share, but we have also been business partners for over a dozen years. While this has been a very successful business partnership, it doesn't mean we don't have to be careful in our communications with each other. Fortunately, we've managed to avoid blamespeak and maintained a healthy, respectful partnership (perhaps because we better practice what we preach!).

In all of these group situations, BIFF communications can help calm conflicts and redirect attention from blamespeak to problem-solving.

## Board of Directors Example

To: Board Members
From: Richard Patel
Message: Election Results

Dear Board Members:

We are pleased to announce the election results for next year's Executive Council seats. First, thank you to this year's Council members for your contribution and leadership. You've guided us through some rough waters, quite successfully.

Below are the members of the Executive Council for the coming year, which begins January 1st and ends December 31st.

- President—Carson Dole
- Vice President—Sidney Kurt
- Secretary—Malia Ortez
- Treasurer—Jack Goldschneider

Congratulations and thank you!

Sincerely,
Richard Patel
Board President

. . . . . . . . .

From: Alana Bigotti
To: Board Members
Message: RE: Election Results

I WAS THE ONLY ONE UP FOR BOARD PRESIDENT!!! HOW THE HELL DID CARSON GET VOTED IN? I DIDN'T KNOW ANYONE ELSE WAS RUNNING AGAINST ME! HOW COULD YOU DO THIS TO ME? I'VE DEDICATED EVERYTHING TO THIS BOARD AND NOW YOU'VE ALL TURNED AGAINST ME! F*** YOU ALL! I'VE LITERALLY DONATED THOUSANDS OF DOLLARS AND DEVOTED HOURS AND HOURS TO YOU! I HELPED ALL OF YOU AND THIS IS HOW YOU PAY ME BACK? I'M DONE!!!!

## Response #1

> To: Alana Bigotti
> From: Richard Patel
>
> Cc: Board Members
> Message: Election Results
>
> Dear Alana:
>
> Carson also submitted his name and the Board elected him based on his board experience and calm management demeanor. I regret that you are so upset about it and I hope you'll calm down before the next board meeting. Call me if you have any further questions.
>
> Rick

## BIFF CHECKER

**Is a response necessary?**　　　　　　　**YES**
She's very angry and will engage others and possibly bad-mouth the organization to the public. If she is continuing on the board, there will need to be some reining in of her anger one way or another.

**Brief?** *(2-5 sentences)*　　　　　　　**YES**
So brief as to be abrupt.

**Informative?** *(who, what, when, where, what for)*　　**YES**
It just has the cold facts of how it happened.

**Friendly?**　　　　　　　　　　　　　**NO**
It feels cold and uncaring. Also, it clearly implies that she does not have a calm management demeanor.

**Firm?**　　　　　　　　　　　　　**MAYBE**
By suggesting that she call him, she may call and yell at him; or she may decide to stay silent since he doesn't sound able to be influenced

on this subject. Sometimes saying that you are open to a phone call implies that you are not defensive at all about the conversation and will not change your position, which often discourages a complainer.

| Advice? | NO |
|---|---|

| Admonishments? | YES |
|---|---|

He says: "I hope you'll calm down before the next board meeting." This feels like a put-down.

| Apologies? | NO |
|---|---|

## IS IT A BIFF?                    NO

While this seems like a BIFF response on the surface, it really isn't a BIFF because it isn't friendly and because of the admonishment.

**Response #2**

To: Alana Bigotti
From: Richard Patel

Cc: Board Members
Message: Election Results

Dear Alana:

Thank you for submitting your name for the Board President position. Carson also submitted his name and the Board elected him based on his board experience.

We very much appreciate your service and financial contributions to the board, and I hope you can support our ongoing work for the benefit of our community.

Call me if you have any further questions.

Best regards,
Rick

## BIFF CHECKER

| | |
|---|---|
| Is a response necessary? | YES |

She's very angry and can get herself and the company in trouble.

| | |
|---|---|
| Brief? *(2-5 sentences)* | YES |

It's just four sentences.

| | |
|---|---|
| Informative? *(who, what, when, where, what for)* | YES |

It explains the outcome of the election without slipping in any negative emotional messages.

| | |
|---|---|
| Friendly? | YES |

It thanks her for submitting her name for the election and also for her service and financial contributions.

| | |
|---|---|
| Firm? | YES |

It doesn't leave any hooks for her to grab onto. Since he offered to have her call him, she probably won't.

| | |
|---|---|
| Advice? | NO |

| | |
|---|---|
| Admonishments? | NO |

| | |
|---|---|
| Apologies? | NO |

## IS IT A BIFF?                                    YES

This is a BIFF response. It is also copied to the board, so that Alana knows that everyone is hearing the full story and will be less open to manipulation by hearing her blaming.

## Family Business Dispute Example

Dear Board Members,

As you are aware, the court has appointed me to serve as an "attorney" member of the board until: the board is stabilized; new members are appointed in the coming year; and the company is consistently in the black again.

138

I look forward to joining you at the scheduled meeting next week.

Sincerely,
Hans Jablonski, Attorney at Law

. . . . . . . . .

Hans—Despite what the "court" in its imperial wisdom has "decreed", you will never be a voice in this company that's been in our family for 87 years. My grandfather started this company. I will never allow outsiders to dictate to us.

Barbara a/k/a Majority Shareholder

. . . . . . . . .

To:      Barbara (Mom)
From:   Kate (Daughter)
Cc:      Jack (Son)

Mom! Stop! Enough! We've been fighting over this for too many years and ended up in court because you fired your own children from our leadership roles in the company and on the board. If you can't get on board with the new structure, we'll never get back in the black and the hundreds of people we employ will lose their jobs. We've lost $150 million since you fired us and we're teetering on insolvency. The new board under the court's instruction is our only hope for survival. I hate to say this to my own mother, but you are the only one to blame for this. Everything was running smoothly until you woke from your drug-induced slumber and decided you were the queen. This is too ugly and I personally can't bear it any longer. You must step aside and let those of us who can salvage this company from the destruction you've wrought—your daughter and your son—to restore and preserve everything that Grandpa and Dad built. For the sake of the company and all of us, you have to either keep quiet or step down. You can no longer treat others, especially Mr. Jablonski, this way. Jack, for Dad and Grandpa's sakes, let's get this right. Can you help me here?

Kate

## Response #1

From: Jack (Brother of Kate; son of Barbara)

To: Kate and Barbara

Mom and Kate: Please stop arguing! Jan is going to be on the board and there is no benefit to us continuing to fight. I'm sorry, but this is ridiculous. It's time to just stop it! It's a good family business, but it's in trouble because we are fighting so much. So just cut it out! Please!

## BIFF CHECKER

| | |
|---|---|
| **Is a response necessary?** | **YES** |
| The family conflict is escalating and needs to stop. | |
| **Brief?** *(2-5 sentences)* | **YES** |
| **Informative?** *(who, what, when, where, what for)* | **NO** |
| There is no new information provided; just arguing with them to stop arguing. | |
| **Friendly?** | **NO** |
| Except he did say "Please!" | |
| **Firm?** | **MAYBE** |
| He tried to stop the arguing, but this is not a calming communication–it may incite them to more conflict instead of less. | |
| **Advice?** | **NO** |

| Admonishments? | YES |
|---|---|

He admonishes them to "just cut it out."

| Apologies? | NO |
|---|---|

However, he says the word "sorry" but it is clearly not as an apology.

## IS IT A BIFF?                    NO

**Response #2**

From: Jack

To: Kate

I know you're frustrated with Mom and so am I. But let's try to calm Mom down by using the BIFF communication method. Remember, our family business consultant said it's better at calming conflicts than venting our frustrations—of which we rightfully have many!

Here's my attempt at a BIFF response to Mom's email. See what you think, if you want to join in on it with me:

Dear Mom,

We know it's been a hard time for you lately and that you care about the business that Dad and Grandad built. We do too and we agree that the best thing to do now is to accept Hans on the board. It will be easier for you and the company to let us deal with the details going forward. It will also help us stay out of trouble with the court.

We want you to be able to enjoy life without having to worry about the day-to-day business. You contributed to building the company with Dad and now it's time for the next generation to grow the business. Know that you are appreciated and that we care about you.

Love, Jack and Kate

## BIFF CHECKER

| | |
|---|---|
| **Is a response necessary?** | **YES** |

Mom is on the verge of sabotaging a court-ordered arrangement to keep the business alive. Kate is on the verge of escalating Mom instead of calming her down. This is a BIFF response (to Mom) within a BIFF response (to Kate).

| | |
|---|---|
| **Brief?** *(2-5 sentences)* | **YES** |

It may be a little long, but it seems to convey the message Jack is trying to send.

| | |
|---|---|
| **Informative?** *(who, what, when, where, what for)* | **YES** |

To Kate he recommends the method. To Mom he explains that it will be easier with Hans on the board and will satisfy the court. (Positive and negative consequences.)

| | |
|---|---|
| **Friendly?** | **YES** |

Jack agrees with Kate on the many frustrations they both have. He makes an effort to calm Mom by appreciating her contributions, saying they empathize with her difficulties lately, and that they care about her.

| | |
|---|---|
| **Firm?** | **YES** |

Jack doesn't leave any emotional hooks to engage Kate or Mom. He says they need to accept Jan to the board.

| | |
|---|---|
| **Advice?** | **NO** |

Jack says that it will be easier for Mom to let them primarily run the details of the business with Hans, but that isn't advice–it's more of a suggestion.

| | |
|---|---|
| **Admonishments?** | **NO** |

| | |
|---|---|
| **Apologies?** | **NO** |

## IS IT A BIFF?                                                  YES

It possibly could be shortened, but it's more calming and persuasive than Kate's response and Jack's initial response.

## Business Partner Dispute Example

Dan: We've been business partners for a long time, which has built trust between us. After an audit of the accounting going back five years, I've uncovered financial irregularities that are concerning to me and that deserve explanation. Our agreement is not clear on expenditures but based on our trust relationship, I understood that we would split office expenses for our business. What I'm seeing is that I'm paying my half, plus your half, plus any other office expenses for your other business. And I see donations to your grandson's baseball team. I didn't agree to that. That wasn't the deal and we need to settle up the difference and determine how much I should be reimbursed.

-Harry

. . . . . . . . .

Harry: Are you accusing me of stealing? I use my cell phone for work—period. I'm not going to split out cell phone expenses between my companies. No time for that. And I thought you were a big fan of helping out young people. Was I wrong? Does it really impact your bottom line? You make plenty of money. As the saying goes, [racial/ethnic slur]!

-Dan

(Unfortunately, this is based on a real case in which offensive language was used. We're seeing more of such prejudiced statements against many different racial/ethnic groups in business, so we will deal with it here.)

**Response #1**

Dan, How dare you speak to me that way! You're ignorant and you know it. This just makes you look stupid.
Now, back to the issue at hand. We need to go over the

expenses and sort them out. You and I can do that or I can do that with the accountant and let you know what you owe. Which is it going to be, a—hole! (I can call names too, you know!)

-Harry

## BIFF CHECKER

**Is a response necessary?**      **YES**
There is the accounting that needs to be dealt with, as well as his racial/ethnic insult.

---

**Brief?** *(2-5 sentences)*      **YES**

---

**Informative?** *(who, what, when, where, what for)*    **MAYBE**
Harry explains that Dan looks stupid speaking that way, and also explains that Dan has a choice about how to approach the accounting problem.

---

**Friendly?**      **NO**
Harry responds in kind to the name-calling insult with a name-calling insult of his own.

---

**Firm?**      **NO**
It has plenty of hooks to trigger a response from Dan. It ain't over yet.

---

**Advice?**      **NO**

---

**Admonishments?**      **YES**
"How dare you speak to me that way."

---

**Apologies?**      **NO**

## IS IT A BIFF?      NO

This is not a BIFF response. (While it is an appealing way to respond to Dan's racial/ethnic insult with another insult, it isn't a good solution.)

## Response #2

Dan, It is no longer socially acceptable to talk to people that way and there are serious consequences when you do. You've said before that it's just an innocent expression, but it's not—it's a prejudiced insult. We're going to lose business and you're going to lose a partner if you say that. So cut it out! You know better than that.

Now, with the expenses we have two choices: We can go over it together or I can do it with an accountant. You decide. Let me know by tomorrow. We should be able to work this out.

-Harry

## BIFF CHECKER

| Is a response necessary? | YES |
|---|---|

There are two problems: the insult and the expenses.

| Brief? *(2-5 sentences)* | YES |
|---|---|

| Informative? *(who, what, when, where, what for)* | YES |
|---|---|

It informs Dan of the risks of using his insult (lose business and a partner) and that he has two choices regarding the expense calculations.

| Friendly? | YES |
|---|---|

It attempts to educate Dan about the risks of his prejudiced insult and ends with a positive, hopeful statement: "We should be able to work this out."

| Firm? | YES |
|---|---|

Harry doesn't put out any hooks to pull Dan back into a fight.

| Advice? | NO |
|---|---|

| Admonishments? | NO |
|---|---|
| Harry does say Dan could lose him as a partner, but it isn't a specific threat or admonishment. | |

| Apologies? | NO |
|---|---|

## IS IT A BIFF?                    YES
This is a good biff response.

### Us-Against-Them Language

Nowadays it is becoming much more common for us to see and hear racial/ethnic insults in some people's blamespeak. This isn't only offensive to the individual hearing or reading it, but it also contributes to a degrading workplace culture. It feeds the us-against-them conflicts that can destroy a business, a reputation, and cause the loss of a good job. While being fired for such a reason these days may bring complaints of cancel culture from the person fired (and their friends), it is important to make the workplace and the whole business a safe place for people of all backgrounds, ages, genders, and beliefs to feel comfortable. In many cases, as in the partner dispute above, someone may be able to be coached in cleaning up their language. In other cases, it is a deal breaker and it has ended partnerships as well as caused lost jobs.

We consulted on a case of a middle level manager in a high-tech company division which had individuals from several different cultures working together. This manager wrote demeaning and insulting emails referring to these cultural differences, seemingly to motivate people on the team. We were asked whether we thought the person should be fired. We suggested that the manager receive coaching in writing BIFF communications, *then decide* whether they could change enough to stay in the job. They liked that idea. We don't know how it turned out. But that general principle is one we encourage:

Coach people to clean up their written language and their verbal language and thinking about others may improve as well.

## Conclusion

In this chapter, we addressed common situations that arise these days with boards, committees, and partnerships. Even some of the most smoothly-run organizations can be suddenly hit with a high conflict person using blamespeak in your midst. We have suggested language that you might use, but it's important to remember that you need to fit it to the situation and your best judgment.

Overall, we recommend using BIFF communications even when responding to crises and insults. It can be tempting to react and over-react when caught by surprise with blamespeak. However, now that you have been warned, hopefully you will not be totally caught off-guard and will give yourself time to pause before responding.

Lastly, remember that you can (should?) get a second opinion on what you have written before you send it. Getting coaching for BIFF communications is the next chapter. Also, when it comes to dealing with board members, committees, and partnerships, get some good legal advice too—before you hit send!

# SECTION 4

---

# Coaching for BIFF

## CHAPTER 11

# Coaching Co-Workers and Others to Use BIFF

Throughout this book we have encouraged you to have your BIFF communications reviewed by someone else before sending them out. This chapter describes our method of coaching someone (anyone) in reviewing their own BIFF communication, so that they can more wisely decide on their own edits before hearing the coach's feedback. This way, the coach can assist their colleague or client in becoming more effective with writing their BIFF communications in the future—even when the coach may not be available.

Anyone can be a BIFF coach for someone else. You may be coaching a colleague at work or coaching a client. (The common term for a person you are coaching is the "coachee.") You may find yourself coaching a family member or friend, who asks for your feedback on something they have written. We regularly hear that people are coaching relatives, friends, neighbors, co-workers and others in writing BIFF communications. We find that most people teach at least one other person how to write a BIFF after they have learned and practiced it themselves.

## The Ten Coaching Questions

We have developed ten questions for reviewing a BIFF communication. Here are the questions to ask someone you are coaching, or to ask yourself if no one is around to coach you:

1. Is it brief?
2. Is it informative?
3. Is it friendly?
4. Is it firm?
5. Does it contain any advice?
6. Does it contain any admonishments?
7. Does it contain any apologies?
8. How do you think the other person will respond?
9. Is there anything you would take out, add, or change?
10. Do you want to hear my thoughts (or someone else's thoughts) about it?

The first seven should look familiar by now. You can review them in Chapter 2. The idea is to ask the person to look at what they have drafted and tell you what they think about it after you ask them each question. At first, just briefly ask them each question, then move on to the next without discussion until you get to question number 9. Then, discuss whether they want to change anything.

If you start discussing any one question in depth prematurely, you may not get to the other questions and something may slip through. That's why we recommend asking all nine questions first. If they start getting into one question, you can tell them: "Hold onto that thought. We will be discussing that soon." That way they get the benefit of looking at the big picture before changing any particular sentence or phrase. This doesn't have to take long at all.

**How will the Other Respond? (Question 8)**

This question is important, to get the BIFF writer to anticipate how their BIFF communication will be received by the specific recipient. It may be easy to picture how the writer would feel getting it. But how will this recipient feel? Can the writer put himself or herself into the other person's shoes? Is the other person a high conflict person, which means they may be easily hooked into their negative emotions? Will it calm the situation? Or is there a phrase that may hook them and escalate the situation again?

**Anything You Would Change Now? (Question 9)**

Now is the time to address the coachees' responses to the prior eight questions. Most often, the BIFF writer realizes that there is something they should take out, rather than add. Nasty comments can accidentally slip into the communication, or unrelated issues. The best BIFF communications are usually the most streamlined, to-the-point-and-you're-done paragraphs. Now's the time to fix it, and the best person to do that is the BIFF writer himself or herself. This is the best way to learn, by responding to these questions oneself.

A common question at this point is whether a certain phrase or whole sentence should be removed. Often coachees will ask the coach for their advice on this. We recommend that the coach hold back on giving their thoughts and instead ask the client first to read it out loud *with* the phrase or sentence, then read it out loud *without* that phrase or sentence. The coachee usually quickly realizes which way is best. The reality we have seen, after coaching clients with hundreds of BIFF communications, is that they usually take it out. Less is more with a BIFF.

If you don't agree with the coachees' assessment of how to write it, then after they have made all of their edits (if any) you have an opportunity with the next question—the last question.

**Would You Like to Hear My Thoughts? (Question 10)**

Now, you can share any feedback that you think is important. Maybe you think it's too long. Or not at all friendly. Or that there's an admonishment in it. Just don't overload your coachee with lots of negative feedback. When people are dealing with a high conflict person, they often feel very vulnerable and often self-doubting. So, don't become another critic in a tough situation. Be as supportive as you can, while also giving realistic feedback. Pick the most important concern you have and discuss that before going onto the next.

After you have given all of your feedback, make sure to tell your coachee: "But, it's up to you!" You don't want them holding you responsible for the outcome after they send their BIFF. The outcome may be out of both of your control, so you don't want to get blamed. You will want them to feel responsible for how it turns out, so that they learn from it and can refine their future BIFFs, rather than depending on you all the time.

## Small Business Owner Example

In this case, a business owner (Sue) developed a close relationship with an out-of-state client (Jennifer) who came to Sue's city for two weeks to work out the details of her design project. The two enjoyed working together on the project and the boundaries of the relationship got blurred. They went out in the evenings and told each other intimate details of their lives. But at some point, Sue realized that the client was becoming too attached and intense and needed to have reasonable boundaries re-instated.

At this point, the client felt abandoned and became outraged. She wrote the business owner the following email:

> Dear Sue,
>
> You have ruined my life! I came to Harrisonburg to help you understand my project needs and you took advantage of me. You led me on to believe that we were close friends and I trusted you with some of my deepest, darkest secrets. I also invested substantial sums ($10,000) in having you work on my design project, but now I no longer trust you. I want my money back. I no longer want you to be the one handling my project.
>
> I also feel that you owe me for the pain and suffering of opening up to you and having you be so insensitive

to me. I am back home now and I am devastated. I am re-living the torment of my childhood abuse, which I discussed with you. I am an open wound that may never be healed. For this I believe you owe me an additional $10,000 dollars for the counseling costs I am going to incur because of my pain and suffering that you caused. (A total of $20,000.) I am wondering whether I need to go into the hospital because of you.

Sincerely,
Jennifer

At this point, Sue seeks coaching on how to respond. She asks another business owner who has been a mentor at times to give her some feedback. Here is the letter that she drafted before her coaching session:

**Sue's First Draft BIFF Response**

Dear Jennifer,

I am so sorry that our business relationship has come to this end. I have examined everything I said and did during your visit in Harrisonburg and I fail to see how I could have possibly led you on to believe that we were close friends. We only had a business relationship from start to finish. Since you were staying here from out of town, it only seemed appropriate for me to have dinners with you since you knew no one here. We did share some important details of our lives, but it always was with the understanding that it was within our business relationship—at least it was for me and I thought you realized that.

I am so sorry that you are hurting and going through such a terrible time. I am thinking that you opened up some old wounds by sharing your childhood experiences with me. I feel so bad about what happened in your life, but I do not feel that I did anything to open up that wound. That was your own doing.

In closing, I easily did $5000 worth of work on your design project before and during the time that you were here. If you truly want me to stop all work on it, then I will refund you $5000. But I think it makes more sense for me to complete the project rather than refund your money. And I won't be giving you anything for pain and suffering and counseling. That is on you.

Let me know what you prefer about finishing the project.

Sincerely,
Sue

## BIFF Analysis #1: Coaching Sue

Here are Sue's answers in response to her coach asking her each of the first nine BIFF Coaching questions:

1.  **Coach: Is it brief?**
    Sue: No, it's probably longer than it needs to be.
    Coach: Okay. Hold that thought and we'll come back to it in a few minutes.

2.  **Is it informative?**
    Sue: Yes. I think I tell her exactly what the situation is. I tell her I'm not responsible for her pain and that I will refund her half the project money, if she wants.
    Coach: Okay.

3.  **Is it friendly?**
    Sue: Yes. I say I'm sorry and sad that she is hurting.
    Coach: Okay.

4.  **Is it firm?**
    Sue: Yes. It ends the upset conversation and focuses Jennifer on a Yes or No question. But maybe I put some hooks out there that will trigger her, such as emphasiz-

ing that I'm not paying for pain and suffering. Maybe I shouldn't say anything about that.

Coach: Okay, hold that thought and we'll come back to it soon.

5. **Does it contain any advice?**
Sue: Maybe. By saying that opening up old wounds was Jennifer's own doing, I may seem to be giving her advice.
Coach: Okay.

6. **Does it contain any admonishments?**
Sue: No.
Coach: Okay.

7. **Does it contain any apologies?**
Sue: Yes. I say I'm sorry our business relationship has come to an end this way.
Coach: Okay.

8. **How do you think that Jennifer will respond?**
Sue: Well, she won't be happy that I'm not giving her money for pain and suffering, and that I'm only giving back half of the $10,000 she paid me.
Coach: Okay.

9. **Now, is there anything you would take out, add, or change?**
Sue: Yes. I'm going to say I'm "sad" instead of "sorry" that things are ending this way, because I truly am sad about this—but I don't believe I did anything wrong.
Coach: Anything else? You thought it might be a little long. You also wondered about emphasizing that you're not paying for her counseling. Why don't you try reading it without that sentence and see which way you like it better.
Sue: Okay. (Sue reads it without the sentence saying

she won't pay for pain and suffering and counseling.) Yes, I think I like it better without that sentence. It is already implied, so I don't need to focus her attention on my negative response to that.

10. **Now, would you like to hear my thoughts about it?**
Sue: Yes!
Coach: I think it sounds defensive and unnecessarily explaining your perspective, so I would suggest leaving out most of the first paragraph and all of the second. Here is how I would suggest doing it, taking into account that you already have decided to remove some words:

**Sue and Coach's Second Draft:**

Dear Jennifer,

I am sad that our business relationship has come to this end. We did some good work together. In terms of a refund, I easily did $5000 worth of work on the design project before and during the time that you were here. So, I will refund you the remaining $5000 and send you my work on the project, if you agree that this finishes the matter.

Sincerely,
Sue

**BIFF Analysis #2: Coaching Sue**

1. **Is it brief?** Yes. It's so much shorter now, but I think it's good.

2. **Is it informative?** Yes.

3. **Is it friendly?** Yes.

4. **Is it firm?** Yes. It asks a Yes or No question at the end. However, it doesn't give a deadline for responding.

Since this is such a sensitive situation, it makes sense to give her room to decide that. Especially since she'll be motivated to get the money back.

5. **Does it contain any advice?** No.

6. **Does it contain any admonishments?** No.

7. **Does it contain any apologies?** No.

8. **How do you think that Jennifer will respond?** Well, she won't be happy, but it doesn't criticize her and is matter-of-fact about the money. I think she'll think about it and then ask for the $5000 and end it there.

9. **Now, is there anything you would take out, add, or change?** Sue: Yes. I'm going to add at the end: "I truly wish you all the best."

10. **Now, would you like to hear my thoughts about it?** Sue: Yes.
    Coach: I think adding your sentence at the end sounds nice. I want to make sure you're okay with the whole thing, because I took out a lot and it's always up to you, as the BIFF writer. Why don't you read it through again and see if you like it. And feel free to add or subtract or change anything before you send it, since it is coming from you. It's always up to you!
    Sue: (Reading it again out loud.) I like it as is, with my extra sentence at the end. I think I'll go with it. Thanks!
    Coach: Good work!

   **IS IT A BIFF? YES!**

### Emotional Boundaries at Work

This example shows what can happen when people get too close to you at work. This is not unusual for high conflict people who may be looking for a much more intense relationship at work than is realistic, since they tend to lose friends because of their emotional intensity. Then, when the inevitable limits get set on them by co-workers, professionals, bosses, or employees, they over-react with anger and possible legal, financial, reputational revenge.

It's better to have clear personal boundaries at work, so that no one misunderstands how close they can get to you. Yes, its tempting to get close because of working closely together, especially on a big project or under an intense deadline. However, its always easier to be clear and consistent from the start to avoid the risk of a situation like Sue had above.

## Conclusion

This chapter has explained how simple it can be to get some BIFF coaching from another person. It is not counseling or legal advice. It is just ten questions that can help the BIFF writer focus on what is important to include and what is important to leave out. If no one is handy to get BIFF coaching from, a BIFF writer can just ask himself or herself the ten questions on their own.

The example with Sue shows in detail how a coach can be non-directive in assisting the BIFF writer in reviewing their communication. By being asked the ten questions, the writer is thinking and learning how to improve their own writing for now and the future. Rather than thinking that the coach is brilliant, the writer gets much of the credit for discovering changes they want to make after thinking about their answers to the questions. This keeps it on the BIFF writer's shoulders, so that the BIFF coach is less likely to be blamed for the response that the writer gets. Remember to always end with: "It's up to you!"

Overall, this coaching process makes BIFF communications simple for anyone to use, while benefitting from another person's perspective when possible. Rather than reacting and increasing the conflict, the goal is to *think* about what to write in an effort to calm the conflict while conveying necessary information.

## CHAPTER 12

# You Decide

A t the start of this book we indicated that blamespeak appears to be increasing in society and especially in our work. Yet we don't have to let blamespeak take over our lives. We can decide how to respond to it and how to prevent it or minimize it from the start—as individuals and as well-functioning organizations. BIFF communication is a very simple tool to turn things around in the heat of the moment and in our overall work culture. Anyone can use BIFF and anyone can coach each other on their BIFF communications.

Using BIFF appears to calm the defensiveness that occurs primarily in parts of the right brain so that we can shift our focus to the logical, problem-solving skills of our left brain. It's not that one part of the brain is better, but that one part is designed to help you survive in a life-or-death situation and another part is designed to solve complex problems that often involve other people. By responding to blamespeak with a Brief, Informative, Friendly and Firm communication, we have chosen to shift ourselves, which tends to shift those we are responding to. We have BIFF work in coaching hundreds of people over the past fourteen years and we constantly get feedback about it calming personal conflicts around the world.

**BIFFs Are Simple, But Take Practice**

Writing BIFFs is simple, but it's not easy and takes practice. In the chapters of this book we have given you over thirty examples of writing BIFFs and a checklist to make sure they are

Brief, Informative, Friendly, and Firm, as well as containing no advice, no admonishments and no apologies (just to be safe that they aren't used against you). By user the BIFF Checker, you can get better and better at spotting language that may trigger the other person unnecessarily. In the back of this book we give you a list of the BIFF examples.

In Section 2, we focused on examples of using BIFF with those external to your organization, such as with customers and clients, and resolving conflicts as ombuds in certain organizations. These are just a few examples, so that you will need to apply the method to fit your specific situation and correspondence. Remember that BIFFs can vary a lot based on the BIFF writer, the reader and the situation. We hope we have not given you the impression that there is only one right way to write any particular BIFF. Use your judgement to fit the situation.

In Section 3, we focused on internal examples, between co-workers, with supervisors and bosses, and with employees. We hope we haven't offended anyone by implying that certain roles or industries have more blamespeak than others. This has nothing to do with the location, the nature of the work, or the organization.

In Section 4, we focused on coaching for BIFF: seeking coaching and giving coaching. As you saw, the structure of the ten questions makes it very easy for anyone to do this. But remember, the coach should not try to counsel or give legal advice unless you are qualified and the BIFF writer has asked for that.

**I Don't Wanna Do It!**

It's natural say "Why do I have to be nice when I'm being treated so badly?" We all have that thought some of the time. But it's important to know that you are a *conflict influencer* in this process and that using BIFF communications can help you make your own life much easier. Sure you could blast them back, but then you might have to spend the next few weeks or months (sometimes years!) trying to make up for it. Remember, BIFFs can save you time, money, and emotional turmoil—especially if you are dealing with someone with a high conflict personality.

## High Conflict Personalities

Who uses blamespeak the most? HCPs. We have addressed the issue of high conflict people (HCPs) briefly throughout this book, who can exist in any location or organization and appear to be increasing in society, perhaps because of our modern culture of blame and disrespect. Keep in mind that personalities are mostly developed as we grow up, so that no one chooses their personality (although we can choose to change it a bit).

While HCPs have not been our focus of attention (because anyone might use blamespeak at any time), we wanted you to know about the blaming behavior of HCPs so that you do not blame yourself unnecessarily. Also, we hope that you will use BIFF at times to help you set limits as needed with an HCP, since they have such a hard time stopping their own high conflict behavior. We have many other resources which speak more in depth about high conflict personalities on our website and in our other books.

## Have Some Empathy

Throughout the examples, you have read some very angry words. In order to shift to using BIFF in response, it helps to have some empathy for the person who is being difficult—even if they have a high conflict personality. Keep in mind that anger is typically a secondary emotion that has a vulnerable emotion under it. For example, in the Threatened Lawsuit Example, Joe Jones was furious, with his lawsuit threat, his capital letters, and intense blaming of his lawyer. Yet after receiving a BIFF response, he responded saying that he appreciated the email and that he felt "obviously lost and in a lot of emotional discomfort."

This is really what is often going on beneath the angry surface. If you choose to respond with some empathy, it often shifts the other person away from their anger. Now, of course, most people won't thank you for your BIFF communication, but they often at least stop fighting with you. In many cases, we see that the other person simply stops making their complaints, threats, or criticisms; which is a great relief to the target of their attacks.

**Reducing Blamespeak in Your Life**

We are surrounded by blamespeak in modern life, on TV, on the radio, on the 24/7 news, on social media, in movies, in website comments and reviews; it's endless. But we can even decide about this. It's possible to reduce your exposure: watch less news, don't comment when it isn't positive or really necessary, don't react to everything you hear, don't participate in unnecessary gossip, and so forth. Sure, its exciting, but is that the kind of excitement that you need?

Instead, go for a walk, talk to a friend or colleague, talk with someone who has empathy, write your negative thoughts and then set them aside, write your positive thoughts and then re-read them, write "I decide" ten times, bake something, listen to music; this list is also endless!

## Conclusion

BIFF is a structure and a tool that you can use to make your work easier and more peaceful. Use your best judgment in making BIFFs work for you. We like to say that our methods are tools, not rules. Let the BIFF structure be your guide. Maybe you would write your BIFFs somewhat differently from the examples we have given you in this book. (Maybe you might have even better BIFFs!) The main thing is to use the four-part BIFF structure and review them using the seven questions in the BIFF Checker.

You can decide whether to escalate or calm conflicts; whether to add to your own stress or whether to take a break and write a BIFF communication. If you can shift yourself, you may be able to shift the person you are communicating with. We have learned that blamespeak can occur anywhere, regardless of race, gender, beliefs or otherwise. In fact, we hope that BIFFs will be used to calm unnecessary conflicts over such differences anywhere at work and in the world.

In short, we want to help you find the missing peace in your work life. BIFF can help.

## List of BIFF Examples

# References

Eddy, B. *BIFF: Quick Responses to High-Conflict People, Their Personal Attacks, Hostile Email and Social Media Meltdowns.* (2014). Scottsdale, AZ: Unhooked Books.

Eddy, B. and G. DiStefano. *It's All Your Fault at Work: Managing Narcissists and Other High-Conflict People.* Scottsdale, AZ: Unhooked Books. 2015.

Schore, A. N. *Right Brain Psychotherapy.* (2019). New York: W. W. Norton & Company.

Teicher, M. "Scars That Won't Heal: The Neurobiology of Child Abuse." Scientific American, 286 (3), 68-75.

# Resources

**Conflict Playbook**
www.ConflictPlaybook.com
Online BIFF training and practice, plus additional courses on dealing with high conflict situations.

**High Conflict Institute**
www.HighConflictInstitute.com
Training, consultation and programs for dealing with high conflict personalities and high conflict disputes.

**New Ways for Work**
www.highconflictinstitute.com/new-ways-for-work
A coaching method to help potentially high conflict employees and managers strengthen conflict resolution skills.

***Hiring Radar: Why Successful Companies Avoid Hiring High Conflict People and How You Can Too***
By Megan Hunter, MBA and Bill Eddy, LCSW, Esq.
www.highconflictinstitute.com/bookstores/hiringradar or anywhere books are sold.

***It's All Your Fault at Work: Managing Narcissists and Other High Conflict People***
By Bill Eddy, LCSW, Esq. and L. Georgi DiStefano, LCSW
www.highconflictinstitute.com/bookstores/its-all-your-fault-at-work or anywhere books are sold.

## Acknowledgements

We could not write a book like this without the help of our team at High Conflict Institute who extend loads of grace as we try to meet deadlines. Thank you for your patience Betsy Johnson, Susie Rayner and Sarah Driver. Bill thanks his wife, Alice, for her endless support and graceful feedback. And thank you to Megan's sweet husband, Paul, who also extends a lot of grace.

## The Authors

**Bill Eddy** is a lawyer, therapist, mediator, and the co-founder and Chief Innovation Officer of the High Conflict Institute. He was the Senior Family Mediator at the National Conflict Resolution Center for fifteen years, a Certified Family Law Specialist lawyer representing clients in family court for fifteen years, and a therapist for twelve years. He serves on the faculty of the Straus Institute for Dispute Resolution at the Pepperdine University School of Law in California and is a Conjoint Associate Professor with the University of Newcastle Law School in Australia. He has been a speaker and trainer throughout the United States and around the world. He has written more than twenty books, including two award winners, and has a popular blog with Psychology Today with over 5 million views. Bill lives in San Diego, California with his wife.

**Megan Hunter** holds an MBA and is a speaker, trainer, and consultant on managing high conflict disputes and challenging people. She is the CEO and co-founder of the High Conflict Institute and founder and publisher at Unhooked Media. She is the author or co-author of five books and has given presentations across the United States and in seven countries. Previously, she was the Family Law Specialist at the Arizona Supreme Court Administrative Office of the Courts and Child Support Manager at the Dawes County Attorney's Office in Chadron, Nebraska. Megan lives in Scottsdale, Arizona with her husband, with whom she raised a blended family of eight children.